TALES TO TELL II

TALES TO TELL
II

by David Campbell

SAINT ANDREW PRESS

EDINBURGH

First published in 1994 by
SAINT ANDREW PRESS
121 George Street, Edinburgh EH2 4YN

Copyright © David Campbell 1994

ISBN 0 7152 0687 7

British Library Cataloguing in Publication Data
    A catalogue record for this book
    is available from the British Library.

    ISBN 0715206877

Typeset in 11/13 pt Garamond.
Cover and text illustrations by Carrie Philip.
Cover concept by Mark Blackadder.
Printed by Athenæum Press, Newcastle upon Tyne

Contents

Foreword

by David Campbell

SINCE putting together the first *Tales To Tell* book, I have travelled to many parts of the world with stories, Scottish stories and stories of Faith and Love. I did not *read* these stories, but *told* them to audiences ranging in age from three to ninety; and whether those folk were American, African, from New Zealand or Australia, they were universally entranced by hearing the stories told. I have become convinced that inside everyone there is a child waiting to hear a story and as the story unfolds in the eye of even the most sophisticated, you can see the child's sense of delight and involvement emerging again. It becomes even clearer why the great spiritual teachers – the Buddha, the Suffi, Jesus himself – told their wisdom in stories. They speak to everyone.

In writing these stories, I have made them closer to the mode of telling so that parents, teachers, uncles and aunts – all those who have to do with the nourishment of the young – could easily read them and then tell them in their own words; for that direct and ancient connection of storyteller and listener is the most potent magic of all.

I have made recordings of six different kinds of stories from this book, available on the cassette *Tales To Tell II*. Apart from the pleasure I hope these will afford to the listener, they can also provide an indication of how a story can vary in the telling and act as encouragement for you to tell it *your* way. The simplest and greatest beauty of storytelling is its individuality and the connection that generates. You'll see it in the eyes of your listener as you tell, whatever age the 'child'.

For any who might be diffident to attempt this, I would exhort you to try it once. Take a story you love and tell it. Then, tell it again. You will need no more convincing of the shared beauty and fun and satisfaction to be found in this relationship.

I can think of no greater testimony to the power of story on the imagination of the young than the following. It was sent to me by Jamie's mother after I'd got home from telling stories in New Zealand. Jamie is seven years old and lives in Dunedin. His real name is Joe Connel. This is his story ....

The Storyteller

JAMIE really liked the storyteller.

They had all come over the park to the library to see him. He was tall and wearing a kilt – like his aunt Cathy said he would be – a tartan skirt with a black leather belt and a shiny silver buckle. He had a leather bag in front too – what was it? Oh, yes – a sporran.

And he had long green socks, each with a red ribbon tucked in near the top.

His hair was long and orangey grey and held in a ponytail. Jamie thought it must be what a lion's mane looked like, when it was out loose.

'My name is David,' said the storyteller. 'I'm a storyteller from Scotland. That's on the other side of the world from here.' And he held his hands up, as if he was holding a globe. 'Right up here,' he added, pointing to the top.

Jamie loved the riddles the storyteller started off with. He said he wanted to know if their brains were working. They were. They guessed all the riddles, even before his aunt Cathy or any of the grown-ups. David said there were some riddles adults never got first.

Jamie loved the stories. There was one about a spider, one about a horse, one about a person who was partly a seal and could swim out so, so far.

David taught them a song about an old banjo, with funny endings on the words. Jamie loved it and sang it all the way back to the centre.

Jamie tried building with the blocks, but the banjo song got in the way of his planning. He went to the water trough and poured and splattered and dripped the water in time to the music in his head.

Then, suddenly, there was a terrible crash. The trough collapsed – it tipped, then landed on the floor with a major crash. One leg broke right off.

Jamie got a fright. Jamie got soaked. His shoes and socks were squelchy, water dripping from the bottom of his trousers.

People rushed to hug him, and wrap him in a towel, and to get mops and sponges and newspapers for the water. 'Quick, quick, before it gets to the carpet.'

Jamie took his wet things off. But he didn't want any of the spare clothes from the just-in-case cupboard. Well, only underpants.

'I'll make my own things,' he said, and went to the making table.

Jamie cut a wide piece of paper and crayoned a criss-cross pattern on it. He wound it around his bottom and sellotaped it so it would stay on. That was his kilt.

He cut a thin strip of paper and coloured it black, with no gaps at all. He held it round his waist and sellotaped it together at the front. That was his belt. Then he cut a shiny silver buckle and stuck it on over the join. He made a little brown bag for a sporran and stuck that on too.

Jamie went to the mirror and looked at himself with his kilt, and his sporran, and his belt with the silver buckle.

He frowned.

He went over to the paints. Jamie painted a long green sock on each leg, with a red ribbon near the top of each.

He went back to the mirror and he smiled.

And he sang the banjo song to his reflection.

When Mum came, she hugged him and his kilt made a crinkly noise.

Jamie stood back.

'Hello,' he said, 'I am Jamie, a storyteller from Scotland.' He held his hands up as if he was holding a globe. 'Right up here,' he said, pointing to the top. I will tell you how I came here .... I was standing by the sea, watching a seal swim out so, so far, when a huge wave came and washed me all the way here. And that is the end of my story.'

That night, Jamie told the riddles and stories to everyone.

Before bed, he hung his kilt, his sporran and his belt with the silver buckle up on his wall.

He washed off both his socks in the bath.

And he hummed the song about the banjo to himself as he went to sleep.

Acknowledgments

I WISH to thank Judith Connel for sending her son's story from New Zealand, Linda Bandelier for the spur of her encouragement to produce this book, and Beth Cross for her creative suggestions and amendments in preparing the manuscript.

I thank you, readers, in anticipation of your carrying the art of storytelling forward into the hearts and minds of our children in your own words and ways.

David Campbell
Edinburgh 1994

THE quotation on page 69 is taken from *The New Testament in Scots*, translated by William Laughton Lorimer (Edinburgh: Southside Publishers Ltd, 1993).

BEGINNINGS

In the Beginning

In the beginning God created the heavens and the earth.
The earth was without form and void,
and darkness was upon the face of the deep;
and the Spirit of God was moving over the face of the waters.

~ GENESIS 1: 1 - 2, REVISED STANDARD VERSION ~

THIS is the story of the beginning of all things. Once before a time, before the beginning, before the beginning of all things, was darkness, everywhere darkness. And on the raging sea that was everywhere, darkness, and then there came … there came a breathing on the dark ocean. In the great darkness the soft breath was the spirit of God and out of the blackness the breath made a voice. It was God's voice, and out of the darkness whispered the words of God, 'Let there be light'.

There was one long moment of silence and then, everywhere was light. Light was everywhere and it was good. It was beautiful. And to make it even more beautiful, God separated the light from the darkness. The time of darkness he called night. The time of light he called day.

And evening passed and morning came and that was the end of the very first day there ever was – day and night. It was a beautiful beginning.

On the second day, the Spirit of God moved on the face of the great waters and said, 'Let these great waters divide. Above them will be the blue sky'. And he waved his great hand and there was suddenly a division – above, there was the blue sky and below there was the great waters. And over the blue sky came evening and then the darkness of night. It was the end of the second day.

Now on the third day, God saw the waters below and the skies above; he looked at this and he felt like a great artist, like the greatest artist of all time, and he looked again and he said, 'Hmm, now, let all the waters be gathered into certain places and these shall be called seas. Then, let the dry land appear and it shall be called – the earth'.

On that day there came a great growling and cracking as the mighty mountains burst out of the sea. Steam and smoke there was – high wild crags burst into being, and long gentle valleys, rolling hills and flat plains. There were gigantic seas that were called oceans and little tiny pieces of water held in the hands of the mountains, beautiful little lochs with dancing rivers running from them.

God, the Great Artist, looked at the earth and the sea and he had a wonderful idea –'I need colour for this,' he said. 'Let there be beautiful green coats of grass and plants covering the places of the earth, flowers of every shade and hue, yellow corn and delightful fruits and trees of every size – from the smallest rowan tree to the giant redwood pine.'

And the earth was covered in wonderful vegetation of every kind and shape and colour. Under the seas waved such seaweeds and plants that you could only imagine in a dream. And God looked and he was pleased. The dark of night came with one stride. It was the end of the third day.

On the fourth day, God looked at the blue skies he had created, he looked at the brightness of day and into the darkness of night and he said, 'Something's missing'.

And so he put the bright hot sun, like a king, into the sky to rule the day; and like a queen, the cool yellow moon to rule the night. And for company, he put the planets, the redness of Mars, Saturn with his ring, Mercury, Venus, Jupiter, Uranus, Neptune and Pluto – and then, all round everywhere, like golden lights, he placed the stars. And he looked and saw that it was a marvel. He was happy. The warm sun by day to make all things grow, and the breathtaking moon and stars by night when all things and every creature could rest.

Evening came – the new sun dipped like a great horse and plunged over the edge of the world. At the same time, the moon and stars, as if on a great see-saw, arose into the dark sky and gave the earth their silent light. It was the end of the fourth day. And God was very happy.

And earth and sky and sea on the morning of the fifth day were beautiful, so still, so full of colour ... and God looked deep into the clear waters of the seas and he said, 'But it's so quiet, it's so still, we must have something that moves. Now, let the waters give birth to swarms of living, moving creatures of every shape and size'.

And so it was – the seas teemed with creatures of every shape from the huge lonely blue whale to shoals of brightly coloured goldfish, from quiet peaceful creatures to lightning barracudas and deadly sharks, fishes galore, more kinds than you could imagine, a whole world of colour and movement under the sea ... minnows, goldfish, cod, ling, mackerel, clownfish ... shrimps, crabs, lobsters, shark, angel fish, trout, herring, haddock ... every kind of fish you could ever dream of.

And then God looked up. He looked into the fresh and empty air. He longed to see colour and movement there too. And so, into the air, he created every bird that ever was. And the air was full of flying birds – swift, swallow, starling, chiff chaff, spoonbill, raven, hawk, flamingo, golden eagle, heron, robin – birds of every kind of feather and colour.

And to see them God laughed with happiness ... to see them dipping and flying and swooping and calling. He blessed them in his heart, he blessed them and said, 'Be fruitful, multiply, fill the waters of the seas and the air above the earth – my fishes and my birds'. And the evening was filled with the songs of birds. And smiling, the big moon rose at the end of the fifth day.

On the sixth day, God looked upon the beautiful earth. He looked in the sky and it was full of beautiful birds ... he looked in the waters and it was full of extraordinary fish, and he said, 'I must make creatures for the earth ... the earth too must have its creatures'. And that day he filled the earth with living creatures from the lowest to the highest – from worms and snakes to long-necked giraffes and mighty elephants. He made the tawny lion, the little teeny fleecy lamb, the big strong rhinoceros, and tortoise with its protective shell, cows, horses, dogs and cats, cheetahs, hyenas, gorillas and squirrels, toads and antelopes, rabbits and ferrets, noisy and silent, swift and slow, large and small – creatures of every imaginable kind, God made.

Then, at the very last, when the whole of the Creation was nearly finished, he made his last and most extraordinary creature of all – a Being just like himself. He created the human Being – man and woman – and he gave them great gifts, these Beings. He blessed this wonderful new creature, and his blessing said, 'Have many children so that they can spread to every part of this earth I have made, because I put you and your children in charge of the growing things, the harvests, the corn, the fruit and the grain. You are to look after them. And the fish and animals, you are to take care of them as well. The earth itself and the seas and the skies are all in your care. I have given you fruit and grain and food in plenty – where you live is a paradise. Be well, be happy and enjoy everything – love it well, look after it well and it will look after you, for it, like you, is beautiful.'

And when the golden sun set in wild splashes of red and purple, and the happy moon rose, God was content. It was the close of the sixth day.

On the seventh day, God looked at everything he had made – at the *whole* universe. It was finished – complete. He rested from all this great work and he put a special blessing on that seventh day. He set it aside as a special kind of day, a day of thanks and rest because he was glad ... he was thankful to finish so great a work and just lie back and rest.

And so he walked on the earth, and he saw the swift flight of the swallow, heard the sweet song of the lark, he smelled the beautiful scent of grass after rain, and he smelled the rose. He delighted to see the wonder of his fishes and his birds and his beasts and to see his human likeness enjoying this earthly Paradise.

He came to a little beautiful stream and there he stopped and saw the sun dappling on the water – glittering, glistening and he put in his hand and felt the smoothness of a pebble. He took it out and held it as the water dropped from it, and it seemed to him perfect and wonderful. One of his own tiny creations.

'This seventh day,' he said, 'I will call it the Sabbath. It is to me as bright a place as the sun, I will call it *Sun*day – and it can be a day for people to enjoy all the beauty of the earth.'

And the sun fell below the hills and the moon rose. It was the end of the seventh day. And God was content and happy with his whole wide world.

4

Into the Long Journey

The woman saw how beautiful the tree was
and how good its fruit would be to eat,
and she thought how wonderful it would be to become wise.
So she took some of the fruit and ate it.
Then she gave some to her husband, and he also ate it.

~ GENESIS 3: 6, GOOD NEWS BIBLE ~

AND so, as you have heard, in seven nights and seven days God had created the universe, the earth, and sky and sea, all the creatures of the ocean, the birds of the air, the beasts of the earth, and last of all he had created a man and a woman.

He thought long and he thought hard before he made these first two people. And he made them in the likeness of himself. And gave them the breath of life. The name of the first man was Adam. The name of the first woman was Eve, because she was the mother of all human beings. In these first days on earth, Adam and Eve lived together in Paradise – the Garden of Eden. They had all the beauty of the earth around them, they ate whatever they wanted to eat, and they ran naked and warm in the sun – happy, innocent and easy like children. They bathed and swam and ate delicious fruits, and they slept with wonderful dreams. It seemed to be perfect. They did not need to give a thought to anything. Everything was provided. But there was one small thing, only one small thing in that garden that God had said they must not touch – one tree, the *fruit* of one tree. Apart from that, they could be carefree and easy from the dawning of God's day to its close. The only thing they were forbidden – the one thing – was to eat the fruit of that one tree.

The tree was a rather beautiful tree. It stood in the very midst of Paradise and on it grew rosy red beautiful apples. The tree also held in its fruit a deep secret, the secret that only God knew. Whoever ate the fruit of that tree would share that secret. But the cost was that they would lose their innocence, and they would forever after know the difference between good and bad – a difference that only God knew at that time. So God had forbidden them to eat an apple of this strangely beautiful and dangerous tree.

'If you eat that fruit,' said God, 'You will die.'

Adam and Eve were like a part of one another. So close were they that they were like one person – although, of course, they were also very different.

Eve was full of curiosity and adventure. She was particularly curious about the mysterious tree in the midst of the garden, the beautiful forbidden tree. She often talked to the creatures of Paradise as she went by, and one sunny day she fell into conversation with the old serpent of wisdom – a canny, clever creature he was, very wise indeed. He was sunning himself by a river and as Eve was passing, he said, 'Well, mother Eve, are you not most content in this beautiful garden? It surely has everything your heart could ever desire'.

'Indeed yes,' said Eve.

'And you can eat anything you like, can you not? The fruit of any of these beautiful trees?'

'Any tree,' said mother Eve, 'but the one in the midst of the garden.'

'And why should that be?' hissed the old snake, with an air of innocence.

'God has said so. We must not even touch it, or we will die.'

'No, no, no, no,' said the wise serpent, 'You will not die. Quite the opposite. Your eyes will be opened. You will see like a God. You will know God's secret. You will be free. You will know the difference between good and bad as God does. You will be able to choose for yourselves. You will be independent. You will be able to do as you like as gods do. You will no longer be ignorant like the other animals here, living the same way, day to day, day after day. Life will be full of adventure if you eat the fruit. I promise you, you will become like a God. And besides,' whispered the wily one of wisdom, 'that fruit is not only beautiful to look at – it is *delicious*. It has a bitter sweetness, more interesting than any other fruit in the garden. It has two tastes at once … try it … oh, and by the way, share it with dear old Adam.'

And Eve did.

She took down a beautiful apple from the tree, told Adam all that the old serpent had said, and together they ate the bittersweet apple of the tree of knowledge. At once! like a flash of lightning! they were changed. Their eyes were opened in a new way and they knew right and wrong … they knew that they were separated from the other animals in the garden … they felt naked and alone and they put on a garment for the first time and they hid in the bushes from God.

In the cool of the early evening, God came walking amongst the trees and little streams and flowers of the garden and called out to Adam and Eve, 'Where are you?'

Adam answered, 'I heard you, God, walking in the garden, but I felt naked and afraid, so I hid'.

God sighed, 'I see you are no longer innocent. You have eaten the fruit of the knowledge of Good and Evil. Why Adam, why?'

'I was given the fruit by the woman you gave me,' said Adam.

'And I by the wise old serpent in your garden,' said Eve.

'You have made *your* choice,' said God. 'You have lost Paradise, you have chosen your own way and so now, at once, you must leave. And the serpent shall spend every day of his life, and his children forever, crawling upon his belly over the earth.'

'And what of us?' said Adam and Eve.

'You will leave this place. I gave you everything, but now you will find the pain of discovery for yourself. You will earn every new piece of knowledge in a long, hard and painful way. You will be at a beginning indeed and much suffering will it cause you. Even in discovering the way to use fire, you will burn yourself many times before you become the master or mistress of flames. And you will hurt and maim and kill and destroy each other before you become master and mistress of love.'

'What will become of us?' said Adam.

'Where are we to go?' said Eve.

'It is in your own hands,' said God, 'You have chosen. It will be painful, but you do not go empty-handed.'

'We are naked,' said Adam.

'We have nothing,' said Eve.

God looked at them both for a long time, these two little creatures, his own, and he said, 'You are still blind or ignorant or you would see that you go from this place with many God-like gifts – You now are utterly different from all other creatures. You have the gift of great intelligence – a gift from me. You have the gift of imagination. You have something no other creature has – the gift of words. You can learn great skills of hand. You can store knowledge. You can build and invent. And above all you can, like God, create new things ... I tell you one more thing .... '

'Yes,' they said.

' ... although you have chosen your own way, you have the gift of my love. I will watch over all your struggles and pain and I will help you. And one day, when you have learned to love as I love you, you may even return to Paradise, to a new Garden of Eden. And ... '

God paused.

'Yes,' they whispered.

' ... one day,' said God softly, 'I will send a very special gift to help you to come back to me, your father.'

'And when ... ' they began.

'No more,' said God, 'Go, leave this Paradise, this Garden of Eden I made for you. Try to become not destroyers, but creators, like me.'

And they went, and he watched the two lonely little figures walk hand in hand towards the east, away from the garden, into their long struggle back to God, the struggle that is still ours today.

The Miracle of Me

Five fingers, five toes
Two eyes, a mouth, and a nose.

~ TRADITIONAL ~

'WAAAH! Waaah! Waaah!' – a bawl, a yowl, a yell, a screech, a scream.
What was that? That was me. Me, at the end of my first journey, a long
journey of nine months in pitch blackness.

I began smaller than the eye can see. I began with nothing, no eyes
to see, no ears to hear, no heart to pump, no lungs to breathe, no brain
to think, no tongue to talk with; smaller than a wriggling tadpole,
smaller than a flea. In the dark I grew ... from next to nothing I grew
... and was carried everywhere in a warm cave of darkness .... And long
after my beginning I grew ears to hear and I could hear ... what was that?
rhythms, sounds ... they were the sounds of my mother's blood, the
pulse of her heart all around me keeping me warm in the cave of darkness in the comfort of her womb ... oh cozy, it was cozy there, warm and
safe ... yes, there I was safe and sound.

There I was safe and sound – an unborn miracle – and then, then out
of the cave of darkness, I was pushed into the light of the world, out of

the dark it was so bright, out of the warmth it seemed so cold. No wonder I yelled and yelled and yelled.

So here I was, a new baby with my own face and what did I know? Nothing. But I was perfectly made – no factory ever made anything more perfectly – five fingers, five toes, all tiny, bright shining eyes, snubby nose, pink ears, red mouth, no teeth but a loud loud voice. A new person in the world – me – just a miracle using lungs to breathe. For the very first time, *my* voice for the very first time.

But that long journey through the dark, that was just the beginning. Now began the journey in the light of day – phew! a really tough journey to find what the real me really is. Oh, I had a lot to learn but I learned fast. Oh ho, no I wasn't slow. I was hungry, and quick as a flash I found a place to feed, warm and full of milk. And so I learned to feed and learned that this big world wasn't such a bad place, after all … indeed not a bad place at all. When I was hungry I yelled and by a miracle I was fed. Oh, yes, these were easy-peasy days, not a thing did I have to do for myself. I was kept warm, fed, clean and cosy … a life of ease, a life of luxury.

But after a wee while I began, you see, to get a bit bored with all this. I wanted to get about the place like the bigger folk I could see around me. So I started, right enough, to crawl about and find things to do. I could throw things about and spill things and that was the beginning of trouble. I found some things were too hot to handle, some too sharp and some just plain unpleasant. But then one day I saw a beautiful big yellow banana way above my head. So what do you think I did? For the first time I stood up on my own two feet, straight up – a miracle! – like the big folk, so I could reach it. I grabbed the big banana and ate it … and another big banana, and ate it … and another … and they were lovely – and I was sick!

So I found I could do things without really thinking much about it – I even began to talk. I tried to talk to the cat and the goldfish. They were beautiful creatures. The fish swam in all its lovely colours but it couldn't talk. When I learned to talk it was amazing – a miracle really, part of the miracle of being me. I could tell folk what I wanted. I could say I was happy or sad or hurt. I could laugh and cry and I learned to sing.

It was great. And I could run and jump and play with other boys and other girls. And paint things, and listen to stories. I was growing up and becoming more and more able to do more things.

I looked at the fish swimming and I learned to swim! I could swim too. I looked at the birds flying in the sky and I wanted to fly – then one day I was taken in an airplane and I was flying. And I thought, this is a great thing, a great miracle really to be a human being and to be me, flying over the world and able to go so many places and do so many things, swimming and flying for a start.

And then there was school. When I'd been here in the world for five long years I went to school and that was good and that was bad. Sometimes fun and sometimes horrible. I began to learn things, lots of things. For instance, I learned that some kids were nice and some were not, some were easy to be friends with and some were just plain dangerous. I got into fights and learned my strength and learned that I didn't like fighting. I learned the hard way – black eyes and bleeding nose, bruised lips – and I decided there were better ways of doing things than spoiling this great face I'd been given, or spoiling the great face somebody else had been given. So me being a bit of a miracle, I learned to talk my way out of trouble. And so I decided I'd be on the side of peace whenever possible.

And of course I learned school things too – like reading. I could look at a page with all these amazing funny black marks on it and suddenly I was in the middle of an adventure, in the deep Amazon jungle in search of a lost civilisation following one valuable clue ... alligators in the muddy water ... monkeys in the trees ... the stab of mosquitoes and who knows what lurking in the shadows. That was great – another miracle – my imagination and a whole world of books.

And I learned I could make things like model railway trains and I could make up my own stories. I could make people happy and unhappy – just me, I could do that. I could steal my sister's doll, pinch her arm and make her cry. Or I could make sure she was safe from fire or water or me. I could even be nice to her.

I learned how to make people laugh and I remember my first joke: What do you get if you sit under a cow? A pat on the head. I thought that was really good, really funny. And it made my sister laugh when she was really unhappy because her friend had left our street. I suppose that was about the time I began to think about God too. And I thought wow, I'm glad God made all this world, and me in it. What luck!

Oh, yes, I'm good at quite a lot of things … and, well, not so good at quite a lot of things too. But I'm really glad I'm here. I think even just little me can do quite a few useful things while I'm on this journey through this world.

I mean we can break things or make things;
Make someone happy or make someone sad,
Be pretty decent or just plain bad,
Give someone something to make them smile,
Or give them a look so they run a mile;
Use words like me to make fun and laughter,
Or use them like swords to bring war and slaughter.

And I bet you didn't expect that I'd turn out to be a poet. I made that poem up. Pretty good eh?

Anyhow, before any more poems or jokes, I've got to go now. I've enjoyed telling you a bit about the miracle of me. That's because I can write, you see. So what about the miracle of you? Could you make a list of all that *you* can do. You'll maybe find that you're a miracle too.

Please do – toodle ooh!

from me,

The Miracle!

Hannah and Samuel

If your faith is the size of a mustard seed
you will say to this mountain,
'Move from here to there', and it will move;
nothing will be impossible for you.

~ MATTHEW 17: 20, NEW JERUSALEM BIBLE ~

LONG, long ago in Israel, in a little town called Ramah, lived a man called Elkanah. He was very rich and in these days if you had enough money and could afford it, you could have more than one wife. Elkanah had two. One was called Penninah and one was called Hannah. Penninah was large and strong and loud and proud. She also had several children. She was never done boasting about them. Hannah was small and quiet and sad and humble, because with all her heart she wanted to have a child, but she had none.

Penninah never let her forget this. 'You're not a real wife. You're not a wife at all. You have no children!' she would gloat.

And now it was the time of year that Hannah hated most. Elkanah took the whole family on a journey up into the hills to the city of Shiloh. All of them went – Elkanah, Penninah and her sons, and Hannah – and they made their way to the great Temple to thank God for all the things he had done for them, for all the things he had given them. Penninah thanked God for her beautiful sons. And Hannah prayed silently and asked God to give her just one little baby.

Then Elkanah roasted the meat from one of his very best animals. He put one piece in the Temple, a gift to God for his goodness to the family. Then he gave one piece to Penninah for herself and another piece for each of her children. To Hannah he gave only one piece, because she had no children. Bless you both he said to his wives. But as soon as he had gone, Penninah turned to Hannah and said, 'One piece, you only get one piece because you have no children. You are a useless wife,' she hissed. 'No children. You have not even given Elkanah one child, no fine strong boys like me. You are good for nothing, a disgrace to your husband, a shame to his people. God has cursed you. He has closed up your womb. You do not even deserve *one* portion of meat. The best for you would be to crawl off into the desert and die!'

Hannah said nothing, but Penninah's tongue stung like a whip and hurt her so deeply that she could not eat, not even the one piece of meat she had. She could not eat or sleep. She curled up outside the Temple and cried. She cried and cried. She was sobbing and shaking when Elkanah came along. He guessed at once why she was crying.

'Hey there, my precious Hannah, don't cry. Don't be sad.'

'I have no children,' she whispered.

'You are as precious to me as if you had borne a whole *tribe* of children,' he said. 'We must accept what God gives us. Be happy my love.'

But Hannah was not happy, she was inconsolable. Nothing could make her happy and one day, after the sacrifice and thanksgiving, she threw herself on the ground in the dust outside the Temple and prayed to God with all the power in her being.

Watching her from his place by the door was Eli, the priest of the Temple, and he heard at that moment this solemn promise Hannah made to God. 'Almighty Lord, look at me, I am your servant. See my trouble and remember me. Don't forget me. If you give me a son, I promise I will dedicate and give him to you for the whole of his life.'

Then silently, only her lips moving, Hannah continued to pray to the Lord for a long time as dark began to fall. With all her heart she prayed and she prayed and she prayed until Eli became convinced that she was drunk.

'Woman! Woman!' he shouted. 'Control yourself! Shame on you, making a drunken show of yourself before the very house of the Lord. Have some respect!'

'I'm not drunk, sir!' she answered. 'I haven't been drinking! I am desperately unhappy and I have been praying, pouring out my heart and troubles to the Lord.'

The old priest came closer and looked at her for a long time, 'You are a good woman,' he said. 'It is in your eyes. Go in peace and may the Lord give you what you asked for.'

'I am praying for a child.'

'Children can be a curse as well as a blessing,' the priest said softly, and Hannah looked up into his eyes and saw they were filled with sadness.

'Yes,' repeated the priest, 'may the Lord give you a child who is a blessing to you.'

'Thank you, sir,' said Hannah, and she went away with her heart strangely light. She ate food and was no longer sad.

'If the Lord grants my prayer,' she said, 'I will give him back to God as a servant.'

After that not even the poisonous tongue of Penninah stung her. And soon that vicious woman had to eat her words for, to everyone's amazement, the Lord answered Hannah's prayer and she gave birth to a fine son.

No one was happier than her husband Elkanah.

'I shall make a special gift to the Temple this year,' he told Hannah. 'Our very best beast.'

'Husband, Elkanah,' said Hannah, 'there is something I must tell you. I made a promise to the Lord that if he blessed us with a child, I would make that child his servant. I wish him to be a gift to the Temple and to God. As soon as the child is weaned, I mean to take him to the house of the Lord where he will stay all his life.'

'Hannah,' said her husband, 'do whatever you think best – I will be content, and may the Lord make your promise come true. I am proud to have such a wife as you.'

So Hannah kept her promise to God. As soon as the little boy was past the time of nursing, she took him back to the Temple, back to Eli, the priest.

'Excuse me, sir,' said Hannah to Eli, 'do you remember me? I am the woman you saw standing here weeping and praying to the Lord.'

'Indeed I remember you well,' said Eli. 'I thought you were drunk because you were praying so earnestly to the Lord for a child.'

'God answered my prayer,' said Hannah, 'and gave me this little boy.'

'Praise be!' said the priest. 'And a fine fine looking lad too. What do you call him?'

'I have called him Samuel because he was asked from the Lord. I wish you to take him into the service of God. As long as he lives he will belong to the Lord.'

'Come here my little lad,' said the priest and took the little Samuel in his arms. 'Oh,' sighed the priest, 'I too have prayed to God for a son that would be strong and good and kind and follow our God.'

'But,' said Hannah, 'do you not have sons of your own?'

'I have,' said Eli, 'but every day they make a mockery of me.'

'I am sorry,' said Hannah. 'Perhaps my Samuel will be like a son to you and to God.'

'Perhaps,' said the good priest, stroking the baby's head. 'Perhaps.'

And that is what happened. Eli brought Samuel up in the Temple as a servant of God. The young lad was happy learning from Eli and became just like a son to him. From time to time, Hannah visited them and brought him on his birthday every year a beautiful robe that she wove herself. Hannah had three more sons and a daughter. God loved his servant Hannah.

Eli was delighted with Samuel, but his own children tormented him. They became worse and worse. They made his life a misery by stealing from the Temple. They bullied poor people and took the offerings of meat they brought to the Temple for God.

'Why are you doing this?' asked Eli. 'You are robbing from the house of God.'

'This meat will do us more good than God,' they laughed and they stuffed their mouths and spat the bones out on the Temple floor – the very Temple where their father was a priest.

'How can you do this? You are the ones who should be serving God. You should be following in my footsteps as priests, not turning God's house into a den of thieves! You are making a mockery of your inheritance!'

But his sons merely retorted, 'We have better things to do than grovel to your God!'

It was Samuel who silently watched all this ... who afterwards picked up the bones from where they had been strewn and washed away the spit. His heart was heavy with sadness for the old man he loved like a father, and troubled at the disrespect shown to God whom he loved even *more* than a father.

But Eli was growing older and weaker and could do nothing to stop his wayward children. He was in despair and his life was moving to a close. His greatest comfort was the company and friendship of his student Samuel who was by now a strong young man. Everyone liked him.

One night the old man was sleeping in his own room in the Temple and Samuel was asleep in a little room nearby. A night-light was burning in the young man's room. Suddenly, quietly, out of the darkness, God spoke his name, 'Samuel, Samuel, Samuel, Samuel .... '

At once the young man rose and ran through to Eli, thinking it was his voice. 'Yes, sir,' he said. 'You called me?'

'No,' said Eli, 'I didn't call you. Go back to bed.'

Again the Lord called, 'Samuel, Samuel .... '

And again Samuel rose and went to Eli and said, 'Here I am, for you called me.'

But Eli said, 'I didn't call, my son. Lie down again.'

Now Samuel did not know that it was the Lord that was calling to him because until then the word of God had been waiting in him like a new baby to be born. Now he could hear the voice of the Lord. A third time the Lord called, 'Samuel, Samuel .... ', and the third time he went to Eli and said, 'You called me. Here I am.'

Now Eli realised that it was the Lord who called, so he said to Samuel, 'Go and lie down and if the voice calls again, say, "Speak, Lord. Your servant is listening".'

The Lord came again, stood there and called, 'Samuel, Samuel ....'

'Speak, Lord. Your servant is listening,' replied Samuel.

And the Lord spoke: 'The sons of Eli are wicked. They bully the poor people, they steal from them and they spit in my face in my house, the Temple. They are not fit to inherit the priesthood. I will choose my own priest. Eli has failed to stop them. I will destroy his family and nothing, no sacrifice or offering, will save them from my terrible destruction. No more is to be said. I have spoken.'

There was nothing but an awesome silence. Samuel lay in his bed until first light. He did not want to get up; he did not want to tell the old man, but at last he rose and opened the doors of the Temple and went through to the priest.

'Samuel, my boy,' said Eli, 'what did the Lord tell you?'

Samuel was silent.

'Don't keep anything from me,' said the priest. 'God will punish you severely if you do not tell me everything, if you do not serve him completely as your mother promised all these years ago – so tell me everything.'

With tears in his eyes, Samuel told his old teacher everything God had said.

'Thank you my son. He is the Lord God and he will do what seems best to him.'

It was not long until God carried out his promise.

War broke out and on the same day both of Eli's sons were killed. When the old priest was told the news, he fell from his stool and broke his neck and at once died. But Eli knew that Samuel, his adopted son, would serve God.

And Hannah lived to see God make Samuel the mightiest man in the land, the leader of his people of Israel, and a wise judge able to discern the path of righteousness. The baby which Hannah prayed for had truly become not only a blessing to her, but to *all* the people of Israel.

Nehemiah rebuilds Jerusalem

The Lord builds up Jerusalem;
he gathers the outcasts of Israel.
He heals the broken hearted,
and binds up their wounds.

~ PSALM 147: 2 - 3, NEW REVISED STANDARD VERSION ~

OUR story today is about a man called Nehemiah who lived a long, long time ago in Jerusalem.

Nehemiah loved his native city Jerusalem. In his heart he gave it many names – Jerusalem, the Holy City, the Eternal City, City of Peace, City of Gold, Rock of Paradise, City of Abraham, City of God. But when our story begins, Nehemiah was far from his homeland, far from his beloved Jerusalem. Jerusalem had been invaded and taken over. Nehemiah, along with many other Jews, had been thrown out of his native land, his own city, and sent into exile in a foreign land – Persia.

By working hard he had done well there – so well, that he now worked for Artaxerxes, the Emperor of that land. He even worked in the Royal Palace in the great city of Susa. But Susa was not Jerusalem and Nehemiah yearned to be in Jerusalem.

One day his brother Hanani came to see him.

'How are things at home, in Jerusalem?' Nehemiah asked.

19

'Bad, bad,' was the reply. 'Bad as could be. The walls are broken down, the city gates are burned. There is no defence against enemies and, worst of all, our people are spat upon and treated like dogs by the foreigners in the city.'

Nehemiah was broken hearted to hear the news of his beloved Jerusalem. Every night and every morning he prayed, 'Oh, God of Abraham, God of our fathers, help our people. Rebuild the walls of your Holy City. Make our people safe.' In his dreams he saw the city safe again surrounded by a beautiful, strong wall of stone.

The heart went out of his work in the palace. Every day seemed long. Jerusalem, hurt like an unprotected child, was always on his mind.

One day he was carrying a silver tray with golden goblets of wine to the Emperor and his wife. The Emperor looked at him closely. 'Nehemiah,' he said, 'I can find no fault in your work. You are one of my most valued advisers, but .... ' He paused.

'Yes, your Majesty?'

'I have been watching you lately,' continued Artaxerxes. 'You look like a man who has suffered some great loss. Have you had bad news of your family? Are you not happy here? Do we not treat you well?'

'Better than I deserve, your Majesty. Truly you treat me well. But I cannot be happy. My brother has told me that my own city, the city of my ancestors, is in ruins. It's walls are broken, its gates burned down. Foreigners spit on my people. It breaks my heart.'

'Well,' said the Emperor, 'what do you want to do about it?'

'I would like to go to Jerusalem so that I can rebuild the city.'

'Very well,' said the Emperor. 'Go.'

At once the Emperor made Nehemiah Governor of Judah and gave him an armed escort of horsemen and a Royal pass to go safely through the neighbouring kingdoms. Nehemiah set out immediately. The journey was long and dangerous, through provinces of people that were enemies of the Jews, ruled by powerful leaders like Sanballat and Tobiah. We will hear more about the deeds of these two venomous rogues later. But at last Nehemiah arrived safely in Jerusalem.

He was devastated to find that what his brother had told him was true, and for three days he watched and listened and walked the streets and waited. Then in secret and at night, with only the moon for a light, he rode out on a donkey to discover how bad the damage to the city walls really was. In these days, a city needed high strong walls to keep it safe from the attacks of enemies. On this bright moonlit night, he could see the ruined wall. Not even the sure-footed donkey could keep its feet in the heaps of rubble and stone that had once been the stout strong walls of the city.

'This is a mess,' said Nehemiah. Even the donkey nodded his head.

'I'll call a meeting of all the Jewish people,' Nehemiah said, and the donkey brayed. He took that as a further sign of agreement, so that's what he did – he called a meeting in the market place and invited all the Jews in Jerusalem.

'Fellow Jews,' he called out, 'Look around you. Look at our city. Jerusalem, the Holy City, the Eternal City, City of Peace, the home of our ancestors. It is in ruins. It's walls are broken. It is unprotected. Let us rebuild it, make it once more fit to be the Holy City, the City of God. Let us rebuild the walls of Jerusalem.'

The people began to chant with him, 'Rebuild, rebuild, rebuild the walls of the Holy City.'

And so the great work, what looked like an impossible task, began. Everyone helped. Priests, officials, merchants, craftsmen, men, women and children – Jews of every age and kind were busy, building.

The walls, stone by stone, day by day, grew. Day by day, a little higher and a little stronger and a little safer.

Two men were watching this with curious eyes. Soon, with *furious* eyes, when they saw how fast and how well the wall was growing. These men were Sanballat and Tobiah.

'I don't like this, Sanballat,' said Tobiah.

'Let us take a closer look, Tobiah,' said Sanballat.

So, one morning, they came down to where the Jews were working. They sat on their fine horses and shouted out to each other so loudly that the workers could hear.

'Look, Tobiah, what do these miserable Jews think they are doing?'

'Oh ho, Sanballat, surely not trying to build with heaps of burnt rubble?'

'What kind of wall can you build with rubble?'

'A crumbling wall,' laughed Tobiah.

'Nothing you could call a wall,' said Sanballat.

'Even a fox could knock it down!'

'Or a cat!'

'Or a spider!'

'Or an ant!'

'Or a puff of wind in the night!'

They roared with laughter, but their eyes were cold.

The workers on the wall said nothing, but, one by one, they put stone upon stone on the wall, so always it grew a little higher, a little safer.

As Tobiah and Sanballat rode away, they lowered their voices.

'We could arrange an accident,' said Sanballat.

'We could arrange an ambush,' said Tobiah. 'If we killed a few of these Jewish workers, the others might not be so enthusiastic to build this wall.'

'If we arranged for one or two to be strangled.'

'Yes, or crushed by a big stone.'

'Or simply to disappear in the night like a puff of wind.'

They laughed cruelly and rode off on their fine horses.

But Nehemiah's men heard about their plots and armed every worker with a spear. From that time they laboured from first light of the sun until the stars came out in the evening. Half worked, half stood guard, night and day.

'We'll need to get Nehemiah himself,' said Sanballat.

'But how?' said Tobiah.

I will send him a letter and suggest a meeting in a quiet suitable place. Then when he comes we will cut his throat and he will be quiet forever. When these Jews have no leader, they will be afraid and do as we say.'

'Good,' said Tobiah, and they sent this letter to Nehemiah:

Dear Nehemiah,

A rumour is going round among the neighbouring peoples that you, Nehemiah, and the Jewish people, intend to revolt against the Emperor and that is why you are rebuilding the wall. We also hear that you plan to make yourself the king and that you have arranged for some prophets to proclaim in Jerusalem that you are king of Judah. His Majesty, the Emperor, is certain to hear about this, and when he does, he will seek your death. So I suggest that you and I meet to talk this over for your own good.

Friendly greetings from Sanballat

Nehemiah saw through the trick and sent only a brief reply:

Sanballat,

Nothing that you say is true. You have invented all of it. Our God protects us.

Nehemiah

Sanballat and Tobiah were furious.

'We will need a little more cunning,' said Tobiah.

'I have a plan, a little plan that might lure the fly into the spider's web,' said Sanballat.

'Yes?'

'Nehemiah has a friend called Shemaiah.'

'Yes.'

'Shemaiah loves money.'

'Yes, yes.'

'If we give Shemaiah enough gold, he will invite Nehemiah to dinner.'

'Yes, yes, yes.'

'When they are dining, Shemaiah can tell Nehemiah that we are coming to kill him.'

'Yes, yes, yes ... then what?'

'And the only escape is to hide in the Holy Temple.'

'Now, wait,' said Tobiah. 'I don't follow you.'

'Well,' said Sanballat. 'No one is allowed to hide in the Temple.'

'Yes.'

'So if the Jews discover that Nehemiah has hidden in God's Holy Temple .... '

'Yes, yes.'

'... Nehemiah would be disgraced, shamed, spurned. No Jew would talk to him, or work for him, or build his wall, and then .... '

'And then,' smirked Tobiah, 'we can attack Jerusalem whenever we feel like it. Take what we like, when we like!'

'Exactly, my friend! Good thinking.'

And so Shemaiah was paid the gold. He invited Nehemiah to dinner late at night and Nehemiah, suspecting nothing, went. When they had dined, Shemaiah leaned over and quietly said to Nehemiah, 'My dear friend, I invited you here for a reason. You are in deadly danger as I am myself. Assassins have been chosen to kill us. Our only escape is to hide in the Holy place in the Temple and to lock the doors behind us. They are coming to kill us and it will be tonight.'

'I am not the kind of man that runs and hides,' replied Nehemiah, 'And do you think that I would try to save my life by hiding in the Temple? You know that the Holy place is for the priests alone. It would be a crime against God to go into that place. I would rather die than do such a thing. God will protect me if it is his will. Goodnight Shemaiah. Pray God's forgiveness.' And with that, Nehemiah walked out alone into the dark of the night.

Nehemiah was safe. Sanballat's last trick failed, for the great day came when the last stone was put on the wall and the last bolt was secured on the last gate of Jerusalem. The Holy City was safe, safe from the likes of Sanballat and Tobiah. And it had taken from beginning to end only fifty-two days.

Nehemiah gathered all the people together to celebrate. His beloved city was safe; once more it could be the City of Peace. He gave thanks to God, shouting from the top of the great new wall:

'You Lord, you alone are the Lord.
You made the heavens and stars of the sky.
You made land and sea and everything in them;
You give life to all.
The heavenly powers bow down and worship you.'

The wall was so big and so broad that the people marched along the top of it, round the whole city, playing in a mighty band of drums, trumpets, cymbals, harps, some singing, some dancing, all rejoicing.

Nehemiah closed his eyes. Quietly he whispered, 'Thank you God.' He opened his eyes. His dream had come true. He looked out on the City of Gold, the Eternal City, the City of God. It was safe, protected by a beautiful strong wall of stone. Nehemiah knew that his work was done.

6

Saul and Samuel

The Lord answered Samuel,
'Do what they want and give them a king.'

~ 1 SAMUEL 8: 22, GOOD NEWS BIBLE ~

MUMBLING – the Israelites were mumbling and grumbling and complaining. 'Every tribe in all the East has a king,' they mumbled. 'Every tribe, except us,' they grumbled.

'We have no king to lead us into battle. People mock us, they laugh at us.'

'God himself is your king,' said their prophet Samuel. 'When you were slaves in Egypt, did he not give you Moses to lead you out of captivity? And then, did God not lead you across the river Jordan and into this land of freedom?'

'Yes. But now,' they grumbled, 'we want to be free, free to choose our own leader, free as other people are free. We no longer need your advice. You are old and your sons who are to follow you are not trustworthy. We want a leader who is strong in battle, a man we can see for ourselves, instead of depending on your invisible conversations with God.'

'I am God's prophet, his voice amongst you,' said Samuel.

'You are past it,' they said. 'We want a king and a king we will have!'

Samuel stood up in their midst and said, 'People of Israel, this I warn you. Choose a king and your sons will fight his battles, will die in his battles. Mothers will weep and you will grind your teeth when you carry their cold dead bodies home for burial. Choose a king and you will be no better than slaves in your own land, slaves to the king you yourselves have chosen. And then, don't think God will listen when you come complaining and whining like whipped dogs!'

'We will have a king,' said the people, and Samuel left. He went away troubled and turned to God in prayer.

And God answered him. 'Listen to the people and all that they are saying; they have not rejected you, it is I whom they have rejected, I whom they will not have as their king. Take them at their word and appoint them a king.'

And Samuel trusted in God's wisdom and waited to be guided by him in appointing this new king.

Time passed, but before long a voice came in the deep of the night, calling his name, 'Samuel, Samuel .... '

He remembered that same voice of God had first called him so long ago when he was but a boy serving God's chief priest, Eli. Then God had foretold of great changes, of terrible wars and of the death of Eli and his sons.

Now God's voice called again. 'Samuel, Samuel, do you hear me?'

'Lord, I hear you.'

'Samuel, I will send you a tall young man from the tribe of Benjamin. That is the man you will anoint as king of the Israelites.'

At that time there was one very small tribe, the tribe of Benjamin. A rich man of that tribe, a man called Kish, had a young, tall, handsome son called Saul. Saul was a full head taller than any other man of the tribe. He was his father's pride and joy.

'Saul,' said his father one day, 'I have lost sixteen donkeys; they have strayed. Take a servant with you and look for them.'

For three days and nights, Saul and his servant searched. They set out in one direction to look for the donkeys. They searched high and low, but no donkeys were to be found. And so they turned in another

26

direction and searched in that region. They searched high and low, but still their donkeys were not to be found. They turned to look in yet a different direction, then doubled back on their tracks to search nearer home, and then further afield again – but nowhere could they find any trace of those donkeys. Finally, tired and dusty at the end of a long, hot day, they stopped by a well just outside a small town. Saul said to his servant, 'Father will be more worried about *us* now than the donkeys. We better return home.'

'Let us try just one more thing,' said his servant. 'Let us ask the Holy man in this town. They say he sees into all things and all places, even the future. Perhaps he could help us to find the donkeys.'

'Good,' said Saul 'but how will we find this Holy man?'

Three girls were drawing water from the well and overheard their conversation.

'The prophet is just ahead of you,' said one of them. 'Today he goes to the hilltop to worship God. You will easily find him.'

Now the Holy man was Samuel, and he was expecting Saul, for it was Saul that God had spoken of when he had wakened Samuel to speak to him.

So, Samuel was waiting – and as soon as he saw the tall young man and his servant approaching, he was sure this was the man chosen by God. Indeed, at that moment, the voice of the Lord whispered in Samuel's ear, 'This is the man I spoke of – he will rule my people!'

Just then, Saul came up to the old man and said, 'Old man, can you direct me to the prophet?'

Samuel looked at him with bright eyes. 'I am the one you are looking for. Tonight both you and your servant will eat with me. As for the sixteen donkeys that were lost for three days, don't worry about them. They are already at home, and you, young man, are the one that the people of Israel want as their leader.'

If the earth had swallowed him, Saul could not have been more astonished.

'But sir, I belong to the tribe of Benjamin, the smallest tribe in all Israel. Why are you saying this to me?'

The prophet looked at him. 'It is not *I* who say it. The voice of God says it. Come with me.'

And he led them into a large room, and he put Saul at the head of the table where a beautiful feast was set, and all in a moment a servant appeared with the choicest juiciest piece of roast Saul had ever seen. This he placed before Saul. It was like a dream and that night Saul was given the best bed to sleep in. At first light, Samuel woke Saul and his servant.

'Now,' said he, 'you must be on your way.' And he led them out of the city.

'Send your servant on ahead. I must speak to you alone,' said Samuel. Saul did as he was bid and turned to hear what astonishing thing this old man would say to him next. As soon as the servant was out of sight, Samuel turned to Saul.

'God has chosen you as king of the Israelites.'

And, taking up a jar of olive oil, Samuel poured it on Saul's head, kissed him on both cheeks and said, 'You will rule God's people and protect them from their enemies. And this very day there will be a sign that what I say is true. Here is what the sign will be – after you have left me, you will meet two men at the tomb of Rachel. They will tell you that your father's donkeys have been found. Then you will travel on until you come to the sacred tree at a place called Tabor. There three men will meet you, one leading three goats, one carrying three loaves of bread and one carrying a skin of wine. These men will greet you and one will offer you two of the loaves. You are to accept these loaves and climb the Holy hill of God at Gibeah.

'Coming down from the high altar at the hill of God in Gibeah, you will meet many prophets playing harps and drums and flutes and lyres and singing and shouting and dancing. Suddenly the spirit of God will take control of you; you will join in the shouting and singing and dancing and from that moment you will be a changed man.

'At last, go on to a place called Gilgal and wait there for seven days. Then I will come and tell you what you must do.'

With these words, the prophet was gone. Saul walked like a man in a dream. His mind was reeling with all that the strange old man had told him, but he did not have far to go before every word that the old man had prophesied came true on that very day.

He came to Rachel's tomb. Two men met him and said, 'Your father's donkeys have been found.'

He travelled on to the sacred tree at Tabor. And, as predicted, three men leading three goats and carrying wine and three loaves met him.

'Take two of these loaves,' said one, and Saul did.

'When you come to Gibeah, climb the Holy hill,' said the other, and Saul remembered Samuel's prophecies.

And when Saul came to the high hill of Gibeah, there were as predicted many prophets making music and singing and shouting and dancing. Suddenly God took control of Saul, and Saul in a loud voice began to prophesy so that people who knew him whispered, 'What has happened to this son of Kish?'

'Has Saul become a prophet?'

'Did you ever see a man so changed?'

And even as they spoke, Saul stopped dancing and shouting and silently walked to the altar on the hill and there he stayed.

After seven days, Samuel called a great gathering of all the people of Israel at Mizpah. Every tribe was gathered there, from the largest to the smallest, a huge throng of people.

'Hear, O people, hear what the Lord God of Israel has to say to his people. Hear the voice of your God –

'My people, I brought you out of Egypt, rescued you from the Egyptians and from all your enemies, but today you have rejected me, and ask me to choose you a king. Then a king you shall have! Gather yourselves in tribes and clans before me, and my faithful servant Samuel will show you the king I have chosen.'

In a strange hush of silence the tribes came forward from the largest to the smallest. Tribe by tribe, lots were drawn, and when the people looked to see which tribe had drawn the special lot, lo and behold it was the very smallest tribe – some would say the least important tribe – the tribe of Benjamin, the tribe, remember, that Saul belonged to. And again the head of each family in the tribe of Benjamin drew lots, and it was Saul's family that again won the lottery. The air crackled with excitement as lots again were drawn, this time for each man in Saul's family. Whispers ran feverishly through the crowd as people tried to guess who would win. Everyone was craning their necks trying to see around their neighbours. Children were raised to their fathers' shoulders. The last lot was drawn, and Samuel held up his hand for silence. In a booming voice, Samuel declared, 'From this family, *Saul* is chosen.'

But Saul was nowhere to be seen. He was in hiding behind the camp supplies.

Out of the silence came the voice of God: 'Here is your king.'

And Saul stood up and came forward amongst the people. A full head taller than any other man, he walked to where the old prophet stood.

'Here is the man the Lord has chosen,' said Samuel. 'There is no other amongst us like him. From this time, he is your chosen king.'

And all the people broke into a great shouting: 'Long live the king! Long live the king! Long live the king!'

Saul looked out over the people he was to rule. Samuel also cast his penetrating gaze over the heads of those he had so long tried to lead in the path of God. And God too looked down upon his people. Perhaps it was only God who was able to see on the fringes of the crowd, those few who were not jumping and dancing in celebration – who instead, were standing still and scowling, mumbling to themselves, 'What way is this to choose a king? Why should *he* be king? We will not follow this so-called king.' Perhaps God smiled a slow, sad smile to himself.

Whether Samuel knew it or not, his work was far from over.

7

David
the Shepherd Boy

'Do not look on his appearance ...
for the Lord does not see as mortals see;
they look on the outward appearance,
but the Lord looks on the heart.'

~ 1 SAMUEL 16: 7, NEW REVISED STANDARD VERSION ~

LONG live the king! Long live the king!'

The Israelites were happy. They had got what they wanted, a king – King Saul. The old prophet Samuel had warned them that they were foolish and wrong to take a king, but God had given them their way and now they had what they wanted. Soon it seemed that the people were wise and right to have their king, to have the handsome Saul lead them, for an enemy called King Nahash, a ruthless man, attacked the Israelites. Saul at once led the besieged Israelites to a great and swift victory.

'Long live King Saul!' chanted the people. 'We were right to demand a king. Our chosen King Saul has saved us!' So it seemed that the people were right and Samuel was wrong.

But then came bad news. King Agag of the Amalekites, with a vast army, was invading their God-given land. Agag was the cruellest and bloodiest tyrant in the east, and sworn to destroy the Israelite people.

'I will destroy every one of them, man, woman and child!' he said.

'Now,' said the prophet Samuel to King Saul, 'you must destroy this man and his people once and for all. Take no prisoners. Not a single one!'

So Saul went to war. He was such a clever general, such a brave leader, that his army won another great victory. But he took one prisoner – King Agag himself!

'You have disobeyed God,' thundered Samuel. 'You have let this tyrant live. Then and there, before the eyes of the people, before Saul himself, the old prophet strode forward, sword raised above his head. King Agag looked up in horror and pled for mercy, but with one fierce stroke, Samuel cut the head from his throat. Agag was dead. Samuel turned then to Saul and loudly said, 'God will find a worthy king. You are not fit ... and your children never shall be king in this land.'

At that time, the person who was to be the future king of Israel was sitting on the ground on a rocky hill above the little town of Bethlehem, patiently watching over his father's sheep. His name was David. He was having a competition with himself. On a rock some ten paces away he had placed ten stones about the size of a man's fist. The competition was between his left hand and his right hand, to see if one was more accurate than the other with a sling. As he let fly with a smooth, round pebble, he imagined that the stone he aimed at was the head of one of his country's enemies. Crack, the pebble hit it and knocked it tumbling off the rock – another dead Philistine.

So intent was he on his game that dark fell, quickly as it does in that land, and the moon rose. Suddenly David was still and alert as a prowling shadow crept, close to the ground, over the hill, stalking a sheep, one of his flock. He could see the moon reflected in one bright yellow eye, a glowing light ... a mountain lion. The sling whirred in the air, the stone flew, the yellow light went out, and at the same instant a howl of terrible pain split the night air. His smooth, round pebble, true and straight, had penetrated the beast's eye, and when young David peered through the gloom he knew it was gone. He took up his little harp and in the dark sang a psalm of thanks to God, in a clear soothing voice – and his sheep grazed on in peace.

The next day, a very strange thing happened to David. He was watching over his flock when a servant of his father's came up the hill and said, 'Your father says you are to come home.'

'Now?'

'Yes, at once. I will watch the sheep.'

Without question David obeyed. When he came to his house there was a strange visitor – an old man with a long white beard and strangely burning eyes. It was Samuel, the prophet, and God had guided him to that house to anoint the future king. All of David's seven brothers were standing there too.

The old man stood before David and looked into his young sparkling eyes. 'All of the sons of this house are strong, handsome young men, but God tells me *this* is the one,' said the old man. 'God looks, not at the outward appearance, but into the heart. Kneel, young man.'

The prophet took a jar of olive oil, poured it over David's head, kissed him on both cheeks and muttered, 'Arise, the Lord's anointed.'

Soon the boy was to get another unexpected summons. King Saul was a tormented man, filled with fears and haunted by demon voices. 'The spirit of God has left you. I am an evil spirit come in its place. You will have no peace. God will choose a new king. You have failed him. Your children never will be kings,' howled the voices.

Saul's beautiful wife, Ahinoam, was broken hearted to see her fine husband broken or raging or whining like a hurt animal.

'What are we to do?' she said.

'Your Majesty, I have heard of a musician from Bethlehem,' said a servant. 'People say that he plays the little harp so sweetly that he could calm the rage of a wild beast.'

The musician, of course, was the shepherd boy, and that is how David came to be summoned by the queen herself to the Royal Palace.

'There is the door to my husband's room,' she said. 'He rages like a wild animal.' As the king mumbled and raved, David played his harp – the sweetness of the music soon soothed the devils and demons prowling in Saul's mind. After a time he came to, and noticed the beautiful young man sitting quietly playing the harp and singing the comforting words of one of his songs to God. The king fell asleep like a baby.

So it was that the young shepherd boy David found himself in the Royal Palace, a companion of the king, like a son to him. But at that time, David did not know, and Saul did not know, that the person God had chosen to be the future king of Israel was already in the palace. And his name was – David. But that is a story for another day.

8

David and Goliath

Everything is possible for one who has faith.

~ MARK 9: 24, NEW JERUSALEM BIBLE ~

SAUL, king of the Israelites, was not a happy man. His mind was often attacked by raging black moods that came on him like thunder clouds. Now his kingdom was invaded by the mighty army of the Philistines. Saul was sure that his God had deserted him. He turned to David whose magical harp-playing could soothe even his blackest moods and said: 'For now return to your father, my boy. I must lead my army against our country's enemies. When the war is over, I hope I can hear your beautiful music. But, David, for now play once more before you go.'

And for his king, David played once more a song for victory:

The Lord God gives victory to his chosen king,
By his heavenly power He gives great victories.
Some trust in chariots of war, some in their horses,
But we trust in the power of the Lord our God.

Give victory to the king, oh Lord.
Answer us when we call.
Give victory to the king!

So, David returned to his father's farm near Bethlehem to look after the sheep. Only twelve miles away, across a wide valley, the two armies of the Philistines and the Israelites faced each other. Three of David's brothers were in King Saul's army.

One day, David's father said to him, 'Take ten loaves and this bag of roasted grain to your brothers where they are camped, and take these cheeses to their commanding officer. Bring me back some sign or token that they are safe and well.'

Long before dawn next day, David set out with the food. Just as the sun came over the hills, he arrived at the army camp.

David left the food with the supplies officer just as the armies were lining up to face each other. He ran to the battle line and found his brothers. As he was talking to them, a giant of a man came out of the army of the Philistines. His name was Goliath. For forty days he had shouted insults at the Israelites and a challenge for anyone to fight him in single combat. David had never seen so big a man. He was nearly three metres tall and covered in bronze armour that glittered in the morning sun. His spear was as thick as a man's arm and had a huge sharp iron blade at its end. A soldier walked in front of him carrying his huge shield.

Suddenly the air was filled with the dreadful sound of his thunderous voice. 'Cowards, slaves of Saul the mad king, what are you doing lined up for battle? Not one of you dares to fight me. For forty days I have challenged any one of you, but you are all afraid, all cowards! Once more I wait.'

In the silence the Israelite soldiers muttered to each other, 'Who could fight such a man?'

'King Saul has offered a bag of gold and the hand of his beautiful daughter, the princess, to any one who dares.'

'Yes, but who wants to be torn apart like a dog?'

David was filled with rage and shouted out, 'How dare this heathen who believes in dead gods defy the army of the living God?'

His brothers heard him and were embarrassed, and said to him:

'What are you doing here? Who is watching the sheep? Have you come to watch the fighting?'

'Can't I ask a simple question?' said David.

Other men had heard what David had said and soon word reached King Saul himself. At once he sent for him.

'Your Majesty,' said David, 'no one should be afraid of this Philistine. I will fight him.'

'No,' said Saul, 'you're scarcely more than a boy. This man has been a warrior all his life.'

'I have killed lions and bears who attack my sheep. I will do the same to this heathen Philistine who defies the army of the living God. The Lord has saved me from lions and bears. He will save me from this Philistine.'

David was so confident that at last the king agreed.

'Very well,' he said, 'but you shall wear the best armour. You shall have mine.' When David, the boy shepherd, was fully dressed in Saul's armour, it was too big and heavy for him. So he took it off and said, 'I will fight as I am.'

Never has there been a fight that looked more unequal. From the Israelite camp the slim figure of an athletic young man picked his way down the slope and from the dry bed of the river chose five round smooth pebbles and fitted one into his sling. The only other thing he carried was his wooden shepherd's crook.

From the Philistine army came the giant Goliath clad in full armour. When he saw his opponent he could not believe his eyes.

'Is this a joke? Do you think I am a dog that you can beat with a stick and stones? Today I will give *your* flesh to the birds and beasts to eat.'

'Today,' replied David, 'the living God will give me victory. I will strike off your head and it is the flesh of *your* body that the birds will peck at and the beasts will devour.'

Goliath was enraged at these words and advanced on David, his eyes bright with fury. 'I will hack you to pieces, impudent boy!'

A hush fell over the two armies as these two ill-matched figures advanced towards each other, a nearly naked boy and a giant in bronze armour. Goliath raised his colossal spear. David spun his slender sling. There was a whirr and a blur as the smooth pebble flew through the air. Like the lion that David had laid low, Goliath did not see its deadly flight. The stone struck the bone of the giant's forehead with a crack that echoed over the whole valley. He toppled and fell face-down unconscious on the ground. Before he could move, David ran nimbly to where he lay, pulled the Giant's sword from its sheath, and with one powerful stroke cut the head from the body. Wild cries broke from the watching armies, cries of triumph and cries of fear.

'That is no boy,' said Saul. 'Such a man is fit to marry the daughter of a king.'

The triumphant Israelites rushed down on the frightened Philistines. When they saw Goliath, their champion, dead on the ground, they ran shouting, 'Surely the Israelites had been helped by a great God.'

On that day the Israelites won a great battle, and all the people sang songs of victory, songs in praise of King Saul, songs in praise of David the shepherd boy who had killed the giant Goliath.

9

David,
King of Judah

I do not trust in my bow
or in my sword to save me;
but you have saved us from our enemies
and defeated those who hate us.

~ Psalm 44: 6 - 7, Good News Bible ~

DAVID, the shepherd boy, had killed Goliath, the giant. David had killed two hundred Philistines with a tiny troop of men. David had married King Saul's beautiful daughter, Michal, and was the sworn friend of the king's son, Jonathon. King Saul was jealous. He wanted this boy David dead.

The truth was that David, the young shepherd-warrior, had done everything in his power to help King Saul, soothing away his terrible fits of madness with sweet music from the harp. Now his reward was that Saul wanted him dead. The king was insane with jealousy. He could never get out of his head the song sung by the women after David had killed Goliath:

Saul has killed thousands,
But David has killed tens of thousands.

It echoed in his head: *'Tens of thousands ... tens of thousands ... tens of thousands.'* It stung, it hurt, it hounded him until he decided he must turn and attack this enemy. So, Saul plotted to have David destroyed. Already he had tried twice to have him killed; twice he had failed – so, more and more, the women's song turned to mocking laughter in his head:

Saul has killed thousands,
But David, David, David,
David has killed tens of thousands,
Tens of thousands, tens of thousands.

There was nothing left for David to do but flee, get away as fast as he could. In tears, Jonathon and he parted, and David made his way into the wilderness to hide. With him went some warrior friends who would not leave him.

'We will follow you to the ends of the earth,' they vowed.

'I will hunt him down even if I have to search the whole land of Judah, stone by stone,' vowed Saul. 'He shall not live.'

In the wilderness David found a cave where he and his men could hide, but he was afraid that Saul in his rage would take revenge on his family. So he sent a message to the nearby king of Moab: 'Please let my mother and father come and stay safely with you until I find out what God's plan is for me.'

So David's parents stayed with the king of Moab as long as David was in the cave.

Meantime he heard terrible news. Saul had slaughtered eighty-five priests that he thought were loyal to David; and now, at the head of a great army, he was scouring the countryside searching for David. Saul would not rest until David was dead!

Secretly, and at great risk, Jonathon came to visit David in his hideout on a hillside near a place called Kish.

'Oh, how good to see you my friend,' said David.

'And to see you,' said Jonathon. 'But are you well enough, living out here in the mountains?'

'Healthy as a mountain lion,' said David. 'And how is your father?'

'Sometimes well, sometimes he broods and paces alone. He knows that God himself means you, David, to be king of all Israel. I cannot believe that my father will harm you.'

'We will see,' said David. And once more the two friends sadly parted.

Jonathon was wrong. The frenzy of Saul's jealousy drove him on, and the ugly voices in his head taunted him again and again.

David killed tens of thousands,
David killed tens of thousands.

With three thousand men, Saul hunted for David. By the strangest chance, Saul's army camped in the valley below the cave where David's men were hiding. It was a long, deep, dark cave and in the heat of the afternoon sun Saul himself came up there alone and squatted in the entrance, out of the sun.

David, silent as a cat, crept up behind the drowsy king, pulled out his sharp sword and, then and there, could have ended the king's life with one quick thrust. Instead David, softly, neatly, noiselessly snipped a piece from the king's robe and retired without a sound into the gloom of the cave. The king knew nothing about it.

When Saul had returned to the valley below, David's voice echoed loud and clear from the hilltop: 'My king, King Saul, look at your robe. Here I have the missing piece cut off with the sword that could have cut off your life when you rested in my cave! I did not kill you, why do you seek to kill me? Why do you hunt your faithful friend? Can you not see that I mean you no harm?'

Tears ran down Saul's face. He saw he was in the wrong. 'The Lord put me in your power today and you did not kill me. Bless you – surely you will be the future king of Israel.' Saul and his army rode home.

Yet the fever of jealousy would not leave Saul. Like a terrible disease it returned again and again, and the voices hissed like serpents in his head and would not be still.

David killed tens of thousands,
David killed tens of thousands.

So once more he went in search of David, driven by the voices to destroy him. The strange thing was that once more God put Saul's life into David's hands. As Saul lay asleep, one of David's men crept up and prepared to stab him.

'Let me plunge my spear through him and pin him to the ground with just one blow,' said the soldier. But David said, 'No, God will take him when he wishes. We will not harm the king anointed by the living God.'

And so, a second time, David spared Saul's life.

But now the life of Saul was soon to draw to a close. His enemies – the Philistines – with a mighty army, once more attacked Israel. And Saul had to go to war to save his country. He himself led his army into battle. However, he was no longer as young and strong as he used to be. And the fighting was fiercest around the brave old king himself. In a rain of arrows he was badly wounded.

He turned to his young weapon-bearer and said, 'Draw your sword and kill me so that these godless Philistines cannot put me in prison and gloat over me!'

The young man was afraid and ran away. So Saul fell on his own sword and killed himself. Meanwhile his son, David's sworn friend Jonathon, was killed as he fought to let one of his brothers escape.

When David heard the news, the news of the death of these two men, he tore his clothes with grief and wept. He had lost his dearest friend Jonathon; and even though Saul had again and again tried to kill him, David wept tears for the old king and composed for both of them one of his most beautiful songs. Here are its words:

Jonathon's bow was deadly,
The sword of Saul was merciless,
Striking down the mighty,
Killing the enemy.

Saul and Jonathon so wonderful and dear;
Together in life, together in death,
Swifter than eagles, stronger than lions.

Women of Israel, mourn for Saul!
He clothed you in rich scarlet dresses
And adorned you in jewels and gold.

The brave soldiers have fallen,
They were killed in battle.
Jonathon lies dead in the hills.
I grieve for you, my brother Jonathon;
How dear you were to me!
How wonderful was your love to me
Better even than love of women.
The brave soldiers have fallen
Their weapons abandoned and useless.
Saul and Jonathon so wonderful and dear are dead.

And so at last the words of the old prophet Samuel came true: 'You are the Lord's Anointed and you shall be the king of Israel.'

David became King of Judah and then the first king of a united Israel. And David was the ancestor of the greatest king of all – Jesus the King of Love. Jesus too was to be born in Bethlehem. But that, as you know, is another story.

Hezekiah and Sennacherib

The Assyrian came down like the wolf on the fold,
And his cohorts were gleaming in purple and gold;
And the sheen of their spears was like stars on the sea
When the blue wave rolls nightly on deep Galilee.

~ THE DESTRUCTION OF SENNACHERIB *by* LORD BYRON ~

A LONG, long time ago — two thousand five hundred years ago —
there lived a king called Sennacherib. He was a violent man, a cruel
man, a man without mercy. He was a great fighter and he had a
mighty army. He ruled over the Assyrian Empire. It was the super-
power of the day, and all the little countries and tribes in that large
Empire had to pay King Sennacherib huge taxes, taxes they often
could not afford.

One nation under this tyrant's power was Judah. It was a small
nation: its king was called Hezekiah. This brave leader stopped paying
the taxes. He knew that sooner or later the terrible army of Sennacherib
would descend upon his people like wolves upon a fold of sheep. He
knew they would be destroyed if he did not protect them.

So the brave Hezekiah made a treaty with the neighbouring kingdom of Egypt. They swore to protect each other and then he made the
walls of his city thick and strong, stone upon stone, thick and strong.

He armed his people and then he attacked the Philistines who supported King Sennacherib.

'King Hezekiah has made a treaty with Egypt, fortified his city's walls, armed his people and attacked the Philistines,' said Sennacherib in a dangerously quiet voice. 'Who is this arrogant mouse? How dare he defy Sennacherib the mightiest Emperor in the world? He and his people, I will punish. I will destroy them to the last man. They will not forget the revenge of Sennacherib. Death to Hezekiah and his people. My army marches tomorrow!'

In gleaming purple and gold, the chariots, horses and foot-soldiers of the Assyrian army, thousands strong, streamed across the plain at first light. They wiped out the Egyptian army. The way was now clear.

'Now, we destroy Judah!' boasted the Assyrian Emperor. 'To the last man.'

And the Judean cities did not wait for long till they saw dust on the plain, then the spears gleaming in the sun, then the purple and gold of the Assyrian horde. The Judeans were like sheep in the folds of their little cities.

The wolf of Sennacherib's anger besieged, battered and destroyed city after city, burned the towns to ashes and murdered everyone living there.

King Hezekiah was amazed and alarmed at the terrible speed of the Assyrian advance. He knew that Sennacherib would stop at nothing to destroy him and his people, and especially the precious city of Jerusalem. The Assyrians never gave up a siege. They would wait, one, two, three years if necessary, to starve the people out and then murder them and ransack and obliterate the city.

The main trouble for Hezekiah was water. 'Our walls are strong,' he said. 'If we had a supply of water we could survive. We can grow food if we have water. We need a safe supply of water, a supply that is secret and safe!'

The news was bad. More and more Judean cities were falling before the merciless wolf. Time was running out as the army of Sennacherib, like a black plague, came closer and closer to Jerusalem, the golden Jerusalem, the Holy City:

The Assyrian came down like the wolf on the fold,
And his cohorts were gleaming in purple and gold;
And the sheen of their spears was like stars on the sea
When the blue wave rolls nightly on deep Galilee.

Jerusalem awaited the attack. Refugees too were flocking into the city in their thousands, fleeing in terror from the revenge of Sennacherib.

'Do not let these people in,' said his adviser. 'We cannot feed *ourselves*, far less those thousands. And how could we survive a siege with so many to feed?'

Hezekiah listened and sighed and said to himself, 'Indeed, how can we feed so many starving mouths?'

But then Isaiah, the prophet of God, came to him and said, 'You must look after these widows and orphans and poor people. Take them in. They too are children of God.' The king did so, until the city teemed with one hundred thousand refugees.

Immediately, when Hezekiah agreed to take in these refugees, he had his most brilliant idea. It came like a sudden flash of lightning in the dark.

'I know,' he said. 'We will divert fresh water from the Spring of Gihon. We will take it underground from outside the city into the heart of Jerusalem. We will dig a tunnel. It will be hidden!'

'Your majesty, it is solid rock,' said his advisers, 'It is five hundred strides long, solid rock. It is impossible to dig such a tunnel!'

'We begin at once. We work night and day. Never a pick or shovel will be idle. One army of diggers will begin outside the city, one within. They will meet in the middle.'

'But how will they meet?' pleaded the advisers.

'They will meet,' said the king, 'and the water will run through this tunnel to our city. This way we will defeat Sennacherib.'

With frenzied speed, two teams started, one from within Jerusalem at the place called Siloam, and the other, outside, at the Gihon spring. They quarried and tunnelled and burrowed as if inspired, and they made a winding tunnel. And as if by a miracle, they met in the middle as the king had said, only fifty centimetres apart. A great stream of life-giving water flowed unseen underground through five hundred metres, out of the dark into the sunshine at the pool of Siloam.

Not a moment too soon it was finished and the dust of the Assyrian army came on the horizon. They had destroyed forty-six cities and now it was the turn of Jerusalem. Sennacherib arrived and his general stood on a cliff opposite the city walls and shouted roughly to all the people: 'Who do you think *you* can trust, that you rebel against the king of Assyria? What good did your God do for the forty-six cities we have destroyed? Our great God Baal spits in the face of your God. Baal gives us victory. He drinks the blood of forty-six cities. No one lives in these cities. Baal the mighty leads us. Your God is dead, dead as you will be unless you surrender. Surrender or you will starve to death and we will throw your bones to the dogs! Hezekiah cannot save you. Nothing can save Jerusalem.'

Hezekiah had commanded his people to give no reply – from the walls of Jerusalem came only silence. However, seeing such a mighty army, thousands of fine horses with purple and gold banners and hundreds of thousands of soldiers, Hezekiah lost heart and went into the Temple and wept. There Isaiah found him and said, 'Be brave, be strong, don't let the king of Assyria and his riff-raff put panic in your heart. We have more on our side than he has. He has human strength but we have the Lord our God to help us. Our God truly is the living God. He will save Jerusalem.'

And time passed and the water flowed silently and secretly into the city while, with endless patience, the Assyrians waited outside. Time passed and time passed and the secret cool water made things grow and kept the people alive.

Endless day after endless day, and still the Assyrians waited. 'They will never go,' King Hezekiah said.

'The Lord has spoken to me,' said Isaiah. 'They will go. Last night the Lord said to me, "King Sennacherib will return by the road he came. Not a man of his army will enter the city. I, the Lord, will defend Jerusalem".'

'I cannot understand that,' said the king.

'You do not need to understand,' said the prophet.

That very night, an extraordinary and eerie thing happened:

Like the leaves of the forest when Summer is green,
That host, with their banners, at sunset were seen:

Like the leaves of the forest when Autumn hath blown,
That host on the morrow lay wither'd and strown.

For the Angel of Death spread his wings on the blast,
And breathed in the face of the foe as he pass'd;
And the eyes of the sleepers wax'd deadly and chill,
And their hearts but once heaved – and for ever grew still!

Opposite the city, the hordes of the Assyrian army crouched and waited. A silent darkness crept over them. The men stirred uneasily. Some groaned in their sleep. A creeping mist hovered over them like black wings of death. Some woke screaming from nightmares and it seemed as if, one by one, they were invaded from within by an invisible and deadly army. They woke pale and fevered and sweating. Some died without even awakening, and when the first pale glow of morning crept over the Assyrian camps, one hundred and eight-five thousand able-bodied man lay stiff and cold and dead:

And there lay the steed with his nostril all wide,
But through it there rolled not the breath of his pride:
And the foam of his gasping lay white on the turf,
And cold as the spray of the rock-beating surf.

And there lay the rider, distorted and pale,
With the dew on his brow and the rust on his mail;
And the tents were all silent – the banners alone –
The lances unlifted – the trumpet unblown.

Not a blow was struck. The rest of the soldiers were filled with terror as they looked into the staring eyes and the silent faces of their dead comrades. They did not wait for the command, nor did they heed the shouts of Sennacherib. They fled as fast as feet or horses would carry them back to Nineveh, leaving Sennacherib to fend for himself. He gazed round at the twisted bodies and the dead faces with their staring frightened eyes. He looked at the horses, foam on their cold lips. He shouted to the skies: 'Baal! Baal! You have failed me! You have let these Jews and their God shame me!'

He took one last look at the limp faded banners, the silent tents, the army of dead men. He wheeled his horse and with bowed head, he rode away from Jerusalem, the jewel that he had failed to destroy. He was a crushed man.

And the widows of Ashur are loud in their wail,
And the idols are broke in the Temple of Baal;
And the might of the Gentile, unsmote by the sword,
Hath melted like snow in the glance of the Lord!

The tunnel of fresh water and the mysterious death angels of God had defeated Sennacherib and the mightiest army of its day.

All this happened two thousand five hundred years ago. Jerusalem was saved, but that was not the end of the story of the city of God. Again and again it was attacked, its walls broken and rebuilt. It was burned down and built up, but always the city that Hezekiah had saved lived again. That wonderful life-giving tunnel of water that saved the city was forgotten, lost, for hundreds of years. No one even knew it was there. But a hundred and fifty years ago, the imagination of the Scottish poet Lord Byron brought the story to life in his poem:

The Assyrian came down like the wolf on the fold,
And his cohorts were gleaming in purple and gold;
And the sheen of their spears was like stars on the sea
When the blue wave rolls nightly on deep Galilee.

Like the leaves of the forest when Summer is green,
That host, with their banners, at sunset were seen:
Like the leaves of the forest when Autumn hath blown,
That host on the morrow lay wither'd and strown.

For the Angel of Death spread his wings on the blast,
And breathed in the face of the foe as he pass'd;
And the eyes of the sleepers wax'd deadly and chill,
And their hearts but once heaved – and for ever grew still!

And there lay the steed with his nostril all wide,
But through it there rolled not the breath of his pride:
And the foam of his gasping lay white on the turf,
And cold as the spray of the rock-beating surf.

And there lay the rider, distorted and pale,
With the dew on his brow and the rust on his mail;
And the tents were all silent – the banners alone –
The lances unlifted – the trumpet unblown.

And the widows of Ashur are loud in their wail,
And the idols are broke in the Temple of Baal;
And the might of the Gentile, unsmote by the sword,
Hath melted like snow in the glance of the Lord!

And in the year 1880, over a hundred years ago, the curiosity of a twelve year old boy called Jacob rediscovered Hezekiah's tunnel. He was playing in Jerusalem at the pool of Siloam. By now the great tunnel of Hezekiah had been long forgotten and lost. People thought the pool was a spring. Suddenly the boy saw cabbage leaves in the pool.

'Cabbage leaves don't float out of springs. Where did they come from?' he thought.

He remembered a spring in the next valley of Gihon, so he hiked up to the spring and found women washing cabbages there!

'Hey,' he thought, 'there must be an underground tunnel connecting the two.' So boldly he went exploring, he went swimming in the spring ... and Jacob, a twelve year old orphan, one hundred years ago, rediscovered Hezekiah's tunnel.

Today, if you go to Jerusalem, you can wade through that tunnel. I have! You start outside the city at the Gihon Spring. You will need a torch because it's black as night. You'd best take a swimming suit too, because the stream that Hezekiah planned is still running. Sometimes it comes up to your thighs and five hundred metres is quite a long way to wade. At least the water is warm. When you come out, you are at the pool of Siloam, the pool that saved the city all those years ago.

Jonah,
are you listening?

*The head does not hear anything until the heart has listened,
and what the heart knows today, the head will understand tomorrow.*

~ THE CROCK OF GOLD *by* JAMES STEPHENS ~

THIS story is about Jonah. He lived a long time ago in the land of
Israel. Jonah was a clever man, a gifted man, a man with great power in
his tongue. He was a wonderful speaker, and when he spoke, it was
said that even the stones would listen. He was also a good man. Jonah
liked God and God liked Jonah. Often Jonah would tell people to live
bright and useful lives because that's what God wanted. Whenever
God asked Jonah to do something for him, Jonah did it. At least that's
what usually happened.

But this story is about a time when Jonah didn't agree with God,
and didn't do what God asked. In fact, he tried to run away. Here's
what happened:

'Jonah, it's God speaking.'

'Yes?'

'Are you listening?'

'Yes, I'm listening.'

'No, you're not listening.'

'No, you're right, I'm not listening,' he laughed guiltily.

'I want you to go to Nineveh.'

'Nineveh?'

'Yes, I want you to speak to the people there. I'm not pleased with them.'

'Nineveh?'

Jonah hated Nineveh. It was full of foreign people, the streets were violent, they didn't speak the same language, they were greedy, they charged high prices to tourists, he didn't feel safe, he could be mugged or robbed. The last place in the world that Jonah wanted to go was Nineveh.

'Jonah, are you listening to me? I want you to go to Nineveh. I'm not pleased with the people there. They're wicked. They've spoiled the city and they're spoiling their own lives. I want you to go and use your beautiful tongue, use your beautiful voice and tell them to mend their ways. For if they do not, I will have no choice but to destroy them and their city.'

'Yes, Lord.'

Jonah heard him, but Jonah was not planning on going to Nineveh. Jonah was planning to run away. So Jonah ran, and he boarded a boat that was bound for Spain so that he could get away from God and this crazy idea of going to Nineveh. Besides he didn't like these people, they were wicked, even God said that.

'They deserve what's coming to them,' he thought. 'Let them be destroyed in forty days. I will be safe in Spain. And safe from God.'

But God knew what Jonah was up to. He knew where he was hiding. Jonah wasn't a good sailor. God smiled. At first he sent a wind, and then a gale, and then a storm. The ship rolled and pitched and tossed and Jonah went green and he groaned, and he skulked below deck and he tried to sleep flat on his back, and he felt awful.

And on deck the sailors saw the storm was getting worse and worse. The ship was in danger of sinking and breaking up. The captain and crew did everything they knew to save the day. They even put all their valuable cargo overboard. They prayed and prayed to their various gods to save them, but everything seemed to be lost and they were in danger of drowning.

Then they remembered their passenger. Jonah awoke, surrounded by the crew, a circle of big burly men.

'Who are you that you can sleep through a storm like this?'

Jonah was only pretending to sleep because the storm terrified him.

'Who are you?' they said.

'My name is Jonah. I'm a Hebrew, and I am running away from my God. He sent this storm because he is angry with me.'

'Your God has sent this storm?'

'Yes,' said Jonah. 'The best thing you could do is throw me overboard. Save yourself, it's no use all of us dying.'

'You're very, very brave, but we couldn't do that.'

And so they tried with all their might to row the boat ashore, they rowed and rowed, but the more they rowed the worse the storm grew. At last they prayed to the God of Jonah, 'Oh God of Jonah, do not punish us, do not punish us for taking this life.' And they threw Jonah into the sea.

And at once, as soon as he hit the water, the sea became as flat and still as glass. The storm stopped, and Jonah plunged down, down, down into the depths of the sea. Oh, there was a dreadful sound of water in his ears. Tangles of seaweed around his hair, thousands of curious fishes all around, and the wreck of ancient ships like white skeletons. He seemed to be at the very roots of the mountains themselves. And he thought he would surely drown.

But God was watching all this, and he had a different plan for Jonah. At that very moment he commanded a huge fish to swallow him up. Along came a great big whale and with one great gulp, it swallowed Jonah. He skited and skidded and slithered, and slid down the slippery gullet, and landed with a thump in the huge, dark cavernous belly of the beast. It was black as night, full of ugsome gases. Jonah was furious. He spluttered and he coughed. He knew this was God's doing.

So, on the first day, he shouted and railed and screamed. On the second day inside the fish, he sighed and wept. And on the third day, he prayed. 'Thank you God,' he said, 'you've saved me from the storm. I've learned my lesson. And I'm sorry. I think you're great, but you've got an odd sense of humour. But thank you for saving me from the storm.'

God was listening. And the moment Jonah said 'thank you', the whale gave a great belch and burp, and Jonah was belched and burped and blown clean out of the whale's mouth, landing on the sandy shore.

He thought he saw the whale give a great wink at him before it vanished into the blue still deeps.

'Now,' said God, 'Nineveh.'

'Very well,' said Jonah, 'Nineveh.'

And so he walked for two days across the desert and then he came to the great city of Nineveh. It was so huge that it took two days to reach the centre. It was market day. Farmers were there with their fruit and grain; women with their stalls of cloth and spices. Why, they looked quite normal.

Jonah stood up on a barrel in the middle of the square.

'People,' he said in his fine voice, 'my God has a message for you. If you do not change your wicked ways in forty days, he will come and he will destroy you and your city.'

No one attacked him. To his surprise, everyone was listening. Even the king came from his throne to hear and when Jonah had finished, he asked Jonah's God to forgive them. The king told his people to fast for forty days. He said they should wear sackcloth and put ashes on their faces as a sign that they were sorry. And Jonah left the city safe and sound, nobody harming him.

Jonah had done what he promised to do. Now he waited for forty days to pass. And the people of Nineveh fasted, and Jonah waited for God to destroy them. On the fortieth day he climbed a hill to see the city burn, to see the wicked place destroyed by God's fire. All day he waited. Night came, still no fire. Jonah was furious. God did not destroy the city. Jonah had kept his part of the bargain – what about God's part of the bargain? Poor Jonah had been thrown about in a storm, he'd been sick, he'd been ill, swallowed by a whale. He risked his life to go to Nineveh, and to talk to the people, and now God was *not* sending his fire to destroy Nineveh. Jonah was so angry that he ran from the hill far, far into the desert. And there he lay down and wept.

Jonah wept until he fell asleep. Now the desert is dangerous. At night it's so cold you can freeze. By day it's so hot you can fry. God knew this. So, in the night, he took out a little seed and planted it by Jonah's head. It was the seed of a gourd tree. And it grew in one night.

When Jonah woke, above him was a beautiful tree. So instead of being fried and frizzled in the sun, he was in the soft green shade. He was cool.

Oh, he looked at the tree, and he loved the tree, but as he looked, before his eyes, it began to shrivel. God had sent a worm into the tree. First the tree grew black, and then it shrivelled and faded, and the leaves fell, and it died, and it was like a skeleton. Once more Jonah crouched on the ground glumfing and glowering.

'What are you doing skulking and sulking, and huffing and snuffling here? What's wrong with you?' said God.

'My tree,' said Jonah. 'My beautiful tree. It's grown brown and black and withered. It's destroyed. It's dead. And you didn't destroy Nineveh. You didn't keep *your* part of the bargain.'

'Stop stamping about and biting your lip and tearing your hair. Sit down a minute and listen. That's better,' said God. 'Ah, Jonah, Jonah … it wasn't your tree; it was *my* tree. And if you're upset about a tree that you didn't even make, nourish or grow, how do you think I would feel, destroying a whole city? And if you can weep for a little plant that was born in one night and died in one day, can you not see how I would weep for the death of a whole city and all its people, its men, its women, its children, its animals? Can't you see that, Jonah? … Jonah?'

'Yes.'

'Jonah, are you listening?'

'Yes,' said Jonah. And he was.

The Plot
against Paul's Life

' ... Lord, I don't know how to speak; I am too young.'
But the Lord said to me, 'Do not say that you are too young,
but go to the people I send you to,
and tell them everything I command you to say.'

~ JEREMIAH 1: 6 - 7, GOOD NEWS BIBLE ~

THERE was never a time that I didn't hear about my uncle. My Mum was always talking about her brother, my Uncle Paul. He was the family tearaway and the family was full of stories about him from as early as I can remember. Mum and he were born in a town called Tarsus, and were brought up to be good religious Jews. Uncle Paul never did things by half, and when Christians began to say that Jesus was the son of God, Uncle Paul went into a kind of fury.

'How dare these people say that this man is God's son! They are blasphemous. They spit on our ancient religion. They should be exterminated. I personally will see to it that we get rid of them. Jail is too good for them. They should be killed off!'

The things he did were terrible. He would not rest night or day from getting these Christians thrown into jail. And he didn't stop at having them killed. It was as if he personally felt responsible for getting rid of them. He fumed and raged and said, 'They are a stain in our land, a blasphemy against our religion and against the true God.'

I remember once he came to our house and told us how he had held their cloaks while a crowd of people stoned a Christian called Stephen to death. He frightened me when he talked about it. A strange glint burned in his eyes and it seemed he would never be at peace until there was not one single Christian left in the land. My mother thought it was like a kind of madness that was in him, like a fever that would not let him go.

Then one day he came to our house and he was like a different man. To me he seemed taller – when I think of it … it was as if he gave off a kind of a glow, yes, as if he was glowing, like a fire.

'I have met Christ,' he said to us. 'I met Jesus Christ on the road to Damascus, and he is the true son of God. I will serve him until I die.'

Well we thought he had gone clean mad. We knew Jesus Christ was dead, executed. The Romans had crucified him. So naturally, no one believed Uncle Paul. How could he have met him?

He told us a strange story. He had been on the road to Damascus and suddenly a great light had blinded him, and this Jesus had spoken to him. He had said, 'Paul, why, why, why are you persecuting me?'

Anyhow, Uncle Paul said he was now going to follow Christ. He was a Christian, and he was preaching the very religion that he'd been trying to destroy. Well, if he'd been energetic before, trying to get *rid* of the Christian religion, now he was twice as energetic preaching and teaching everywhere. He said that this Jesus was the one true son of the living God. And to tell people that, Uncle Paul travelled everywhere, like a person with the strength of ten men. He never seemed to tire.

As I was telling you, I was always hearing stories about my Uncle Paul. In a way he was a hero of mine. But a time came when I became a part of one of the stories, in fact I saved my uncle's life. I'll tell you how that happened.

We were living in Jerusalem at this time. Uncle Paul had been on one of his long preaching journeys in foreign lands, but plenty of news and rumours about him got back to Jerusalem, stories of him being in prison, being stoned almost to death like Stephen, and of him healing people and gathering, everywhere he went, followers for Jesus.

My mother was worried sick about him when we heard that he was coming back to Jerusalem. It was the most dangerous place he could come to. There were still Christians who were suspicious about this man who had been their sworn enemy, the religious Jews hated him for betraying their religion, and the Roman army was nervous and jumpy.

At that time the Romans occupied our country and kept control by force. The Romans were quick to deal with troublemakers, and Uncle Paul was a troublemaker. So, naturally, my mother was anxious for her favourite brother and she couldn't help remembering that the last time Jesus had come to Jerusalem, the Jews and Romans between them had crucified him. And now here was her brother Paul coming to the same city, openly saying that Jesus was the son of God. There was bound to be trouble.

Things turned out just as badly as she expected. As soon as Paul arrived in the Holy City, some Christian friends came to meet him. They warned him that the Jews were out to get him, because the Jews believed he had spoken against the people of Israel, against the Law of Moses and even against their Holy Temple. Well, of course Paul denied this and he went to the Temple to show how he respected the Law of Moses, but the Jews dragged him onto the steps and set on him like a pack of wolves. He would have been torn apart there and then, but the Roman commander sent his soldiers to break up the riot and rescue Paul because he wanted to find out *why* the crowd wanted to kill him.

The soldiers had to carry Uncle Paul above their heads to stop the crowd from pulling him to pieces. All the time the crowd was shouting, 'Kill him! Kill him! He is not fit to live!'

The Romans took Paul off to prison and I thought that he would end up like Jesus, being tried and crucified. I cried myself to sleep and poor Mum looked like a ghost. She was sure we had seen him for the last time.

The whole town was in a fever. In the narrow streets, little groups of men were muttering and plotting, and everywhere the Roman soldiers moved people on. No one knew what would happen next. Because, at this time, I was only a boy of eleven, no one took much notice of me – that is how I was able to save my uncle's life.

I was sitting against the wall of one of the narrow streets eating an orange for breakfast, when some men sat down in the courtyard at the other side of the wall. Then I heard words that made me cold to the bone. It was a man's angry voice.

'I make this vow,' the man said. 'I will neither eat nor drink until we have killed him. The Romans are fools. They do not understand our ways. They may easily let him go. Best that we make sure of him ourselves.'

'Let us *all* make that vow,' said another voice.

I felt gripped by ice and was suddenly sure that they were talking about my uncle, when my fears were confirmed by voice after voice repeating the vow, 'I will neither eat nor drink until we have killed Paul of Tarsus.'

I counted forty voices. Forty men determined to kill my uncle. I listened to every syllable they said and the words stayed in my heart as if they had been branded there with a hot iron. Then I ran to the fort where Paul was a prisoner. We were allowed to visit Paul and I told him everything I had heard.

'They are going to get the commander to bring you down to the council of the chief priest and the elders ... and then ... then when you are on your way through the streets ... they will ambush you and kill you!'

'Now, take your time,' said my uncle. '*Who* is going to ask the commander?'

'The chief priest ... the chief priest and elders.'

'Yes, and *what* are they going to ask him?'

'They're going to pretend they want you at the council, so that they can question you ... but you'll never reach there. They'll kill you first!'

'Hmm, we'll see,' said Paul. 'We'll see, my lad.' He patted my head.

Then my uncle called a guard. 'Take this young man to the commander. He has something to tell him.'

At once I was led through the long stone corridors of the fort to the commander.

'The prisoner Paul,' said the guard, 'called me and asked me to bring this young man to you. He has something to tell you.'

Suddenly I was afraid of this big Roman commander. I had seen these men ordering people to be whipped and crucified, and at that moment all my courage vanished. To tell you the truth, I was on the edge of tears.

'Here, my boy,' said the commander quietly, 'you must be about the same age as my own lad. Come over here and tell me what it is you have to say' – and he led me by the hand to where no one else could hear us.

So I told him … blurted it out all at once. 'The Jewish authorities are going to ask you to take my uncle down to the council tomorrow. They'll pretend that the council wants more accurate information about him. Don't listen to them because there are more than forty men and they'll be hiding and waiting for him. They have taken a vow not to eat or drink until they have killed him. I heard them. They're ready to do it and all they're waiting for is your decision. Don't listen to them!'

The commander smiled, 'Don't tell anyone what you have told me. Now, run along, and not a word.'

I can remember all that as if it was just today. And that's how I saved my Uncle Paul's life – because the commander gave him a huge armed escort to the town of Caesarea. There were two hundred soldiers, seventy horsemen and two hundred spearsmen as well as a horse for my uncle to ride himself. So Uncle Paul was saved.

I never saw a blinding light as my uncle did on the way to Damascus, but I think God made sure that I was sitting eating an orange in the exact spot where I could hear that plot against his life. And I suppose that is one of the reasons that I followed in my uncle's footsteps and became a follower of Jesus as well.

13

Paul's Sea Journey
to Rome

For a number of days both the sun and the stars were invisible
and the storm raged unabated
until at last we gave up all hope of surviving.

~ ACTS 27: 20, NEW JERUSALEM BIBLE ~

MY name is Julius. I spent my life as a soldier and I was in the crack regiment of the Roman army – the very best, the Emperor's Regiment. I had been in Israel for years putting down rebellions, keeping peace amongst the Jews. That wasn't easy – they were a tough, troublesome lot.

Now at the time I'm going to tell you about, I was an officer in the Emperor's Regiment. We were stationed on the coast in a town called Caesarea, named after our Emperor. I liked Caesarea. It was warm; we could bathe in the beautiful Mediterranean. It wasn't like the hot desert or that crowded dangerous city of Jerusalem. Life was easy. Then I got orders to take a prisoner called Paul to Rome to be tried by the Emperor himself.

I didn't like that kind of work. Fighting was one thing – I was trained for that. But taking poor devils of prisoners in chains bothered me and they often enough ended up hoisted onto a cross to die. What

I had heard about this Paul didn't sound hopeful either. Wherever he went, he caused riots. He was a follower of a man called Jesus that we had crucified in Jerusalem as a troublemaker, even though the evidence seemed pretty thin. Now that this Jesus was dead, he had more followers than when he was alive.

So I wasn't looking forward to this journey to Rome by sea. To tell you the truth, I was never a good sailor. Fighting an army with ten to one odds against us was more welcome to my stomach than a rough sea. But then came my first surprise. This Paul came aboard the boat smiling. He greeted me not as if I was his jailer, but a friend. There's some people that you take to at once and he was one of them.

Our first day at sea was as calm as I'd ever seen it and I fell into conversation with the prisoner. We soldiers like a good story and he had an amazing story to tell. But the most amazing thing to me was that this man had been beaten almost to death, he had been stoned, people had plotted to kill him – but he said the way to victory is to love these people, *love* them. I couldn't believe my ears. He said that when this Jesus was dying on the cross, he said, 'Forgive them Lord, for they know not what they are doing.'

Anyhow, when we put into port the first night, I trusted this man. I took off his chains and let him go ashore to visit his friends. He didn't betray my trust and came back on board in good time for us to set out again on our journey to Rome.

This time the weather turned bad. I don't know if you've ever been sea-sick, but I can tell you that days of sickness in a wild sea is my idea of torture. So I was not looking forward to the journey. But we sailed down the more sheltered side of Cyprus and Paul told me more of his story and more about this man Jesus that he followed. It was then that I began to notice something about Paul. He was not afraid of anything in the world – not the sea, not even death. I also noticed something else – the weather was getting worse, the ship was pitching and rocking but I was so intent on his story that I wasn't sea-sick. That for me was a miracle as amazing as any that Paul was telling me about. At last we put into a port called Safe Harbours and there we should have stayed.

It was the end of September and usually the beginning of rough weather. Paul said to me and the captain, 'From here on our voyage will be dangerous. If we continue there will be a great loss of cargo and life.'

That's where I made a big mistake. I listened to the advice of the captain and the ship's owner. They said, 'This man doesn't know the sea. The weather is set fair. This is not a good port to winter in. Let's sail while we have a good wind.' And so sail we did.

A sweet soft wind blew us along and even my delicate stomach could not complain. We made good and easy progress along the coast of Crete. Then there came a little darkness into the sky and a few large drops of rain and then a whispering in the air and a kind of coldness. Then, as if thrust from underneath, the ship began to tug and pull and rock and pitch forward like a frightened horse. But none of this Paul seemed to notice. He was telling me about the moment that the sky darkened when they crucified Jesus ... and at that moment, suddenly, a black storm was on us like a devil let loose from hell, and the waves were roaring and gnashing their teeth like monsters ready to swallow us.

It was terrifying. I would rather have been on any battlefield in the world. In the eerie light I could see the sailors, those that could stand, heaving cargo into the sea to make us lighter, but still we were taking in water and listing badly. For days we could not see sun nor moon nor stars and, at last, we gave up all hope of being saved.

In the midst of all this, and above the terrible noise of the wind and waves, Paul stood up and shouted out, 'You should have listened to me! But men, I beg you, take heart! Only the ship will be lost. Not one of you shall lose his life. For, last night, an angel of the God I worship came to me and said, "Don't be afraid Paul, for God wishes you to stand before the Emperor – so before the Emperor you will go. And God in his goodness will spare the lives of all who sail with you". So, men, take heart.'

By now I believed Paul, but some of the sailors took him for a crank, a madman. As soon as they thought we were near shore they tried to lower the ship's boat and escape. But Paul said to me, 'Officer ... Julius ... if the sailors don't stay on board, we have no hope.'

So I ordered my soldiers to cut the life-boat ropes and let the boat go. So now we had no way off the ship. Slowly a light began to break through the darkness and we could see the sun dimly through the clouds. It was the beginning of a new day.

'Gather round,' said Paul. 'For these past fourteen days when you have eaten nothing, I assure you not even a hair of your heads will be lost, so eat some food.' So Paul took some bread, gave thanks to his God before us all, blessed the bread in the name of Jesus, broke it and began to eat. Every man of the two hundred and seventy-six who were on board ate and then we threw the rest of our cargo of wheat into the sea.

By now it was light, and suddenly, breaking through a sea mist, we found ourselves not far from shore, with a stiff wind blowing us towards the land. The sailors raised the sails to hurry us forward into a bay. We were no more than two hundred metres from land when the ship ground into a sand-bank and then the back part of the ship began to break up into pieces in the violence of the waves.

My soldiers were getting ready to kill the prisoners to prevent them from swimming ashore and escaping. This I forbade. It was my task to make sure that Paul got to Rome to stand before our Emperor. I ordered all those who could swim to try for the shore and those who remained were able to cling to spars and broken parts of the ship. Paul and I were the last two to struggle up onto the beach out of that angry sea.

As we reached the shore, he said to me, 'Julius, do you know what happened to Jesus after he had been crucified?'

'No,' I answered.

'After three days he rose from the dead,' he said.

Yes, he was a strange man that Paul, still telling his story of Jesus amid all that danger. But, you know, not a single man from that ship was lost – a miracle I'd say. And an even greater miracle for me was that not once on the journey was I sea-sick. I think it was because I was so taken up listening to Paul's story.

But, to get to the end of my story. You'll be wondering if I got Paul to Rome? Well, yes I did – but not before two more strange things happened. The people on the island where we had landed (it was called Malta, by the way) were very friendly, very hospitable. It got very cold so they lit a fire to warm us. Paul gathered some sticks for it. Then there was a sudden hush. The heat of the fire had brought out a deadly snake and it twined round Paul's hand.

'This man will die even though he has escaped the sea,' I thought.

But Paul merely shook the snake off into the fire, continuing his story as if nothing had happened.

'And do you know what, Julius? After Jesus was dead and had risen, he sent his Holy Spirit into his followers. It came into them like a fire of courage.'

All this time the islanders were waiting for Paul to fall down dead, but he came to no harm whatsoever.

The other strange thing that happened on the island of Malta was that Paul cured a man who was dying, and before we left he cured many more sick people on the island.

'I cure these people in the name and through the power of Jesus,' he told me.

So that was the story of our journey – me and my friend Paul. Yes, I'm proud to call him my 'friend'.

Paul got to Rome. He lived there for two years, always telling his story. And a funny thing – I've *never* been sea-sick since that journey.

LIVING AGAIN

14

The Cripple
and his Friends

Faithful friends are life-saving medicine.

~ ECCLESIASTICUS 6: 16, NEW REVISED STANDARD VERSION ~

THREE fishermen were mending their nets by their boat on the
shores of the Sea of Galilee. It was a beautiful evening. Their hands
worked quickly and skillfully, patching tears and holes with twine.
They were, even while they worked, deep in conversation, so deep that
they did not notice the figure of Big John, the old skipper with his
sailor's swaying walk, approaching along the shore.

'The way I see it is this,' Philip was saying: 'Nobody else has been
able to cure Zachariah. He's not been able to walk or work or move
from his bed since the day the storm did for his back – a tragic day
and no mistake .... '

'Ach, he was a fool! He should never've gone out!'

Philip was interrupted by the gruff voice of the old skipper who
was leaning on his stick watching them. 'Keep these lines tight!' Big
John warned one of the young fishermen. 'Aye, he should never've left
the shore. He was warned. All the signs of a storm were in the sky.'

He waved his stick over the sea at the sun dipping behind the mountain. 'Just like tonight. I warned Zachariah myself. A storm's on its way, and I can see it now – the wind'll race down the Golan Heights. The sea will be like a wild animal. The very same as the day of Zachariah's shipwreck.'

The three fishermen stopped working. The old man sniffed at the air. 'Mind you, it's more than his back that keeps Zachariah in his bed.'

'What d'ye mean?' asked Danny, the youngest fisherman.

'Something else broke in him that day, that's what I'm saying. Maybe it was his nerve.'

'Away,' said Philip, 'he was the bravest and best of us all.'

'That I know,' continued old John. 'He hurt his back, right enough, but he'll never get over the loss of his boat. And more than the boat ... his *own* son was drowned in the wreck. A fine lad. And that's when Zachariah lost his reason for living. I wish I thought different, but Zachariah'll never get over it.'

'That's just what we were talking about,' said Amos, a man who usually spoke very little. 'A cure for Zachariah. We thought we'd take him to this healer man, this Jesus from Nazareth. He's been teaching and preaching all round the country, but he got back to Capernaum yesterday and he's staying with Peter's mother-in-law.'

'Well,' said the old skipper, 'this Jesus must be a most remarkable man, right enough. I mind how Peter and Andrew and James were fishermen, just like us, and along comes this same man and says, "Follow me" – and they up and followed him, without as much as a backward glance. He's surely got a silver tongue on him.'

'The whole country's speaking about him,' said Amos.

'He's a great healer, they say,' added Philip.

'But Zachariah has been paralysed for years,' John sighed. 'Every doctor's cure and medicine they've tried and he's never a wheen better. How could this man do what no doctor has done?'

'He's cured a man with a withered hand in the synagogue on the Sabbath ... so I've heard,' said Philip.

'Aye,' agreed Amos. 'And when the Pharisees heard that he did it on the *Sabbath*, and in the *synagogue* too, they nearly died of heart attacks and apop ... apop ... apo*plexy*,' stammered Amos in his enthusiasm.

66

'Aye, aye, but d'ye really think *he* could help Zachariah?' asked young Danny.

'Well, he just might, if we could get anywhere near him,' said Philip. 'The last time he was here in Capernaum, he stayed at the same place – mind? – and Peter's mother-in-law was sick with a high fever. I mean, he cured her and she was up dancing attendance on them as frisky as a spring lamb. But word's got about and you can't get near the place for folk waiting to hear his stories – he's a great storyteller. And if it's not the stories, then they want to be cured of everything from leprosy to madness. Even that Roman Centurion went walking all the way up to Cana to ask him to cure his servant – and the lad recovered the very minute Jesus said he would. He's got an uncanny power, right enough, but the problem would be *how* to get Zachariah in to see him. We'd have to carry him in a stretcher and I doubt we'd get near.'

All the fishermen fell silent. The sun's last rays made a red fan above the mountain. A cool breeze touched their cheeks.

'Ye'd better get yer nets down, boys,' said John. 'The storm's coming in.'

'Aye, lads, lower away!' ordered Philip.

And as Danny and Amos scrambled to lower the nets from the high poles where they hung, a white jagged flash of lightning suddenly tore the sky and a crack of thunder shuddered the air.

'Mind how you go lads!' shouted old John. 'We don't want ye falling … more hurry, less speed.'

'Wait a minute!' yelled young Danny. 'Hey, ah know what we could do, we could lower Zachariah into the house the same way we lower these nets.'

'Ach, dinna be daft!' cried Amos. 'How could we do that?'

'Easy – make a hole in the roof!'

'Hurry up and get that net down!' shouted Philip. 'Watch yerself and never mind your blethers!'

'Aye, well … ' pondered big John as the first splashes of rain fell. 'Ye know, there just might be something in what the young laddie says. That would be a way of doing it, right enough. Listen, ye can all count on me. I'd do anything for Zachariah. He's a good man. Aye, aye … down through the roof, that's not a bad idea at all.'

'It's quite a notion, right enough,' said Philip, 'but what would folk say? What would *Jesus* say?'

As darkness deepened round the Sea of Galilee, the four men talked excitedly, thinking and planning. Soon they left their boats drawn up upon the shore.

Zachariah had four visitors that evening. It was very late in the night by the time they left, and the storm had passed over. Between the old pain in his back and the new hope in his heart, Zachariah slept little. The plan of his friends the fishermen was daring and frightening.

From his bed in the sleeping town of Capernaum, Zachariah watched the big full moon slide across the sky. It seemed to laugh. He thought about this man Jesus. Then he shifted to ease his back and wondered if he would be laughing tomorrow. Jings, maybe he would *even* be able to ... no, he hardly dared think about it.

The sun was hardly up when throngs of people gathered in the house of Peter's mother-in-law. Inside, every face was turned towards the man, Jesus, their eyes straining in the gloom. So intent on him were they all, that no one saw four strong fishermen make their way along the roof tops, carrying their crippled friend, Zachariah, on a stretcher.

'If you have faith,' Jesus was saying, 'your father God will protect you. His face will shine on you with the light of love. Ask and it shall be given to you.'

Suddenly, there was a rending and tearing above the heads of the people – a crack and another crack. A whole section of the roof was lifted off and the golden rays of sunlight streamed into the dusty room and lit up the figure of Jesus. Smoothly four pairs of rough, expert hands lowered their crippled friend down on the stretcher. The crowd made a space and there, plumb in front of Jesus, lay Zachariah.

Even Jesus was astonished as he looked up through the gaping hole in the roof. The crowd waited as if in the calm before a storm. A smile broke on the face of Jesus and then he began to laugh. He looked up at the fishermen and down to their paralysed friend. Long and deep, he looked at Zachariah and saw in his face not just the pain in his back, but an *inward* pain that no one else saw. And then, to everyone's surprise, Jesus said, 'My son ... don't be afraid ... your sins are forgiven.'

Two men, officials of the synagogue, were muttering in a dark corner. Like a flash of lightning, Jesus turned and said directly to them,

'I hear what you are thinking. Tell me, which is easier to say to this paralysed man – 'Your sins are forgiven?' or 'Lift up your stretcher and walk?' But just to let you see that the Son of Man has authority from God to forgive sins on earth .... ' He paused, turned once more to the crippled Zachariah, and said gently, 'Get up, take your stretcher and go home.'

The whole of the people of Capernaum and the surrounding country were amazed by Jesus and the wonder of God. The story of how Zachariah lifted his bed and walked spread like a fire on everyone's tongue.

And by the shores of the Sea of Galilee that evening, there were *five* fishermen sitting, talking softly, by the quiet water. Zachariah was one of them and he could walk again.

Here is the same story as it is told in the Bible, from W L Lorimer's *New Testament in Scots*:

Efter some days he cam back til Capernaüm. Wurd gaed round at he wis back hame, and siccan a thrang gethert at there wis nae mair room for them, no een about the door. He hed begoud preachin tae them, whan fowr men cam wi a blastit man carriein on a matrèss, seekin him. Whan they faund at they coudna win forrit til him wi their friend for the hirsel o fowk, they tirred the pairt o the ruif abuin whaur he wis staundin, an loot doun the matrèss wi the blastit man lyin on it throu the hole they hed made. Seein their faith, Jesus said tae the man, 'My son your sins is forgíen.'

Nou, the' war some Doctors o the Law sittin by an thinkin intil themsels, 'What wey can the chíel say sic a thing, na? It's aivendoun blasphemie! Wha can forgie sins, binna God alane?'

Jesus read aff their thochts like a buik, an said til them, 'What wey hae ye sic thochts in your hairts? Whilk o the twa things is aisiest – tae say til the blastit man, 'Your sins is forgíen', or tae say til him, 'Staund up, tak up your matrèss, an traivel'? But tae gar ye ken at the Son o Man hes the richt on the yird tae forgíe sins' – an here he turned tae the blastit man an said til him, 'Staund up, I bid ye, an tak up your matrèss an gang your waas hame.'

At that the man stretchit til his feet an immedentlie tuik up his matrèss an gaed awà afore the luiken een o them aa. They war aa fair stoundit an glorified God an said, 'Ne'er saw we the like o that!'

~ MARK 2: 1 - 12 ~

15

The Roman Officer at Capernaum

But now I tell you: love your enemies
and pray for those who persecute you.

~ MATTHEW 5: 44, GOOD NEWS BIBLE ~

MARCELLUS had been fighting for the Roman army for nearly twenty years. He'd fought in every kind of territory and in every kind of climate – in freezing snow on the mountains and in hot sun in the desert. When he was just a young man, he was tough, fearless and loyal, so he made many friends among his fellow soldiers and caught the eye of his superior officers. He was quickly promoted and became ~~at length~~ a centurion, the officer in charge of a hundred men.

Looking back now, he couldn't remember how many campaigns he had fought, how many prisoners he had taken, how many friends he had seen dead and buried, and he couldn't remember how many times he had escaped death himself on land or sea, by sickness or the sword.

Yes, it had been a hard life. And now here he was in Israel and in charge of the Roman garrison at Capernaum, a little fishing village on the Sea of Galilee. He hadn't looked forward to this post. There was trouble there. The Jews didn't like the Romans – and hated especially the Army and the soldiers. Everywhere there were rebels determined to get rid of the Romans – roving bands of extremists who believed that this was God's own country. They would rather die than serve a foreign power.

One of the centurion's jobs was to organise and supervise the crucifixion of some of these poor devils. That wasn't a soldier's work, that wasn't fighting – Marcellus hated the thought of it. You always had to be on the look out and you never knew in the narrow streets on a dark night when a knife would slip between your ribs; there were tales of soldiers who had mysteriously drowned in the Sea of Galilee, and stories too of a new powerful leader of a band of Jews, another troublemaker. So no, he hadn't looked forward to being in Capernaum.

But Marcellus found that he liked the little fishing village by the Sea of Galilee. The town was neat and pleasant. The climate was good. There was fine fish and fresh fruit in abundance.

The simple fishing people were hardworking and, like most people who know the strange power of the sea, had a deep belief in their God. Soon he got to know many of these Jews; he grew fond of them and loved to talk to them about their way of life and especially about their religion. When he found that their church was in ruins, he even gave the money to have a new synagogue built for them. He was above all a fair man and soon had many friends in the small town. Unlike many of his fellow Romans, he even made a great friend of his personal servant, a man called Sigurd, who had been taken prisoner during a German campaign. They had been together for many years and Marcellus treated him with every kindness, just like a friend.

Marcellus was also a very curious man and when rumours of the great new Jewish teacher came to his ears he decided to find out more about him, for two reasons. First, it was his job and duty as an officer in the Roman army to make sure that this man who attracted a huge following of people, was not a military threat to the might and authority of Rome. This could be the leader many Jews were looking for to rid their country of the hated occupying army.

The second reason for his interest in this great teacher was that Marcellus himself was very curious about God. He could not believe in the dozens of gods the Romans had, and he was attracted by the talk and belief among the Jews of the One God.

He also heard stories of miraculous cures that this new teacher had carried out. He was said to have cured people who were paralysed, people who were mad, even people who were crippled from birth. These miracles were the talk of the land and now this man had made his headquarters in Capernaum – the headquarters of Marcellus' own military garrison. [army]

This very afternoon the [his] teacher was to talk to a huge gathering on the hill above the little fishing town. Word had spread like fire and people had gathered from all over the country to come and hear this Holy man. This Holy man's name was Jesus.

Marcellus dispatched a small, but elite, patrol of his troops to disperse among the people and report to him on what happened and what was said.

It was hot and still on the mountain that afternoon when Jesus spoke out words that would burn through the world hotter than any sun. The great Teacher knew well just who was in the crowd listening – Jews who wanted him to be their soldier-king, Roman soldiers, spies, jealous Jewish officials who wanted him dead, as well as ordinary people of the land, fishermen, farmers, tradesmen, and women with little children. They listened in amazement. None of these people could believe their ears.

'Love your enemies,' he was saying. 'Do good to those that hate you, bless those who curse you and pray for those who ill treat you.' These sounded like the words of a madman. Perhaps the heat had turned his head.

That night Capernaum was a hubbub of chattering about Jesus and his astonishing sermon from the mountain above the village. Marcellus listened quietly to these reports, retired late to bed and for a long time lay awake thinking about what he had heard. At last he slept and in the night fell into a strange dream – he was a young soldier in battle again, and a fierce enemy came at him in hand-to-hand combat. He had his attacker by the throat and was just about to choke the life from him, when a soft voice came floating through the air to him with the words, 'Love your enemies … love your enemies … love your enemies.'

In his dream he loosened his grip on the man's throat and at that moment heard a terrible groan. He woke in a sweat and heard again the deep groan. Suddenly he realised it was his servant in the next room.

Sigurd was scarcely able to breathe, scarcely able to move, paralysed in some way, so that he was too weak even to speak. Marcellus quickly loosened his servant's shirt.

All through the night a doctor attended him, but in the morning the old doctor shook his head, 'He will not live the day out.'

Marcellus could not keep the tears from his eyes. Then he began to think about the man Jesus.

He called together some of his Jewish friends from the synagogue and asked them to find Jesus and ask for his help. They found him easily in the village square, surrounded as always by people. They told him about their friend, the Roman officer, and his sick servant. 'He really deserves your help,' they said. 'He is a good man, he loves our people ... why, he himself built a synagogue for us.'

At once Jesus said, 'I will go and help him', and he went with them.

Well, many members of the crowd muttered and mumbled about this latest scandal.

'A Jew visiting the house of a foreigner! A Roman soldier at that!'

'Why, he should *know* it's against the law of our religion!'

'The Romans are our enemies. What's he doing helping one of *them?*'

The centurion's friends were not far from the house when Marcellus came to meet him.

'Sir,' said the officer, 'I do not deserve to have you come to my house. Just give the order and my servant will get well. I have authority over forces of soldiers and when I say to this one "Go!", he goes, or to that one "Come!", he comes – but you have authority over invisible forces. If you but say the word, my servant will be well.'

When Jesus heard this, he was amazed and he looked round at the crowd following him. He knew full well who was there – the ordinary folk, the curious, the Jewish officials looking for some means to trap Jesus, hopefully to get rid of him forever. There were also the Roman spies.

Jesus said to them all, 'I have never in all this land found such faith as this man has. Some of you, some of you, countrymen, think that you will sit in heaven with Abraham and Isaac and Moses at the right hand of God. You won't! But I tell you, people like this man Marcellus, this Roman centurion, will!'

Jesus could see the Jewish officials squirming; he could see their resentment and he could hear their minds already plotting for his death. They were furious.

Then he turned to the centurion and said, 'Because of your faith, your servant will be well.'

It was exactly mid-day – the sun was at the top of the sky.

The centurion bowed and thanked him and went on his way home. He had not reached his house when many of his servants came rushing to meet him, shouting, 'Sir! Sir! Sigurd, your servant ... Sigurd is well!'

'And was it at noon when he recovered?' asked Marcellus in delight.

'Yes, sir,' they said, amazed at his knowledge. 'Yes, at noon! He asked for a glass of water and he arose from his bed. It was exactly at mid-day that he rose. The sun was directly overhead.'

'Yes,' said Marcellus, 'at noon. I knew he would be well. The healer, Jesus, said so.'

The Tax Collector
at Jericho

*He heals the broken hearted
and binds up their wounds.*

~ PSALM 147: 3, REVISED STANDARD VERSION ~

SMALL, small, that was the trouble – Zacchaeus had always been small. He had been a fine plump little baby alright, but then when all the other boys and girls in Jericho had sprung up and grown tall, he stayed small. He was the smallest boy in the neighbourhood and the others made fun of him; they called him 'titchy', 'short legs', or 'mouse'. So Zacchaeus didn't have many friends. He didn't like people and they didn't like him.

But if Zacchaeus was small, he was far from stupid. In fact he was *very* clever and at an early age he decided that he was going to become rich, so rich that he could do what he liked. He would show these folk who called him names who was the biggest fool. He would have the largest house in the town and it would have its own swimming pool!

And Zacchaeus did become a rich man, and he owned nearly the largest house in the town and it had its own swimming pool. The only larger houses belonged to his Roman masters.

75

Rich, yes, Zacchaeus was rich, one of the richest men in Jericho. He was also one of the most detested men in Jericho because he made his money by collecting taxes from his fellow Jews for the hated Romans.

Zacchaeus was greedy and ruthless. He forced the Jews to pay three and four times the proper amount and pocketed the rest for himself. He had two 'protectors' as he called them, and if any poor Jew fell behind in his taxes these ugly characters, on some dark night, would visit him and break one of his bones to encourage him to pay. Or worse, they would threaten his wife and children. Zacchaeus had grown up to be a small and friendless little man.

One night, he knocked at the door of a poor little house. A pale frightened woman shuffled to answer it. Seeing it was Zacchaeus, she burst into tears. 'You know my husband is blind. He has been begging in the market and on the streets, but we have not enough money to buy food, not enough to live.'

Zacchaeus looked at her. 'You have one week to find the money. I will return in one week at this time. And if you do not pay me then ... it will be the worse for you.'

'But, sir .... '

'One week!' He turned on his heel and was gone.

In a narrow street he came to a house that he hated to visit. It was the house of a leper, a man with a skin disease. Zacchaeus remembered the man's hollow eyes, the scabs and white flakey skin on his face, and shuddered. He knocked and stood back. Once again he heard a shuffling and the door opened. The leper's wife stood there trembling when she saw who it was.

'Sir,' she said, 'please do not ask us for money. My husband cannot work; you know everyone avoids us. He has to carry the leper's bell to warn people of his disease .... '

'Pay!' said Zacchaeus.

'Sir, we have not the money.'

'You have one week,' said Zacchaeus, 'or else!'

'But *sir!* .... '

'One week!' And once more he was gone, leaving the woman leaning against the door in tears. A week passed and once more Zacchaeus stood at the door of the blind man's house. He knocked and heard a firm step walk to the door. It swung open and the man blinked at the light and said, 'Ah, you are the tax collector? I've been expecting you. Here is your money.' And he handed over a purse of coins. 'You'll find that is correct, sir,' he said. 'I counted it myself.'

Zacchaeus was speechless. He looked at the man. 'You can *see*?!'

'Yes, I can see,' said the man, 'and I have earned this money. I am the happiest man on earth.'

'But how did this happen?' said Zacchaeus.

'The great teacher Jesus healed me. He took mud from the earth, spat upon it, laid it on my eyes, and now I am cured. I can *see*. No one could be richer than I am now.'

Zacchaeus was amazed.

Almost before he realised it, he arrived at the house of the leper. He hesitated and then knocked. Once more he heard firm steps, no shuffle, come to the door. There before him stood the leper. Zacchaeus sprang back as if whipped.

'Don't be afraid,' said the man, 'I've been expecting you. Here is your money. It's alright, I've counted it myself.'

Zacchaeus peered into the man's face. He couldn't believe it. Where once the eyes were hollow and glazed, now they were bright and warm. The skin of his face, once scabby and flakey, was fresh as a baby's.

'What happened?' asked Zacchaeus.

'I am cured!'

'Yes, but how?'

'The great healer Jesus, healed me. There were ten of us and we were outside the town when Jesus came by with his friends and followers. I had heard of this great teacher and shouted out to him from a distance, "Jesus, master, take pity on us". He looked at us and said, "Go and let the priests examine you". No one could believe it. When we got to the Temple and showed ourselves to the priests, every one of us was cured, just as I am now.'

Zacchaeus was dumbfounded. 'But who is this man who looks after the blind and diseased?'

'Some say he is a prophet, and some that he is the Messiah, the son of God himself. But I tell you he is the kindest and best man that ever lived. If God is like *him,* I believe in God. This man loves every-one.'

'Everyone?' thought Zacchaeus. 'Ah, but ... he couldn't love me. No one loves me.'

Out loud, Zacchaeus said, 'And where can you find this man?'

'He will be in Jericho today,' said the healed man.

'He will walk down the main street, I am sure – for already great crowds of people are gathered there waiting to see him and to hear him and to be healed by him. Listen, you can hear the crowds shouting. He is like an angel of God.'

Zacchaeus walked away slowly. He felt alone and small and ugly. He could see the hatred in the dark eyes of the people who looked at him. Yet, he found himself drawn to the main street, to where the great crowd was, to where Jesus was to pass.

The murmuring grew like leaves scuttling in the wind. 'He is coming!' chanted the crowd.

Zacchaeus would be able to see nothing. He was small, small, that was the trouble. Even on tiptoe he would see nothing. So he ran ahead of the crowd and there by the roadside he saw a sycamore tree. It had branches that he could climb easily and they leaned out over the road. He scrambled up the tree to hide and wait. From here he could see this extraordinary man and no one would know he was there. As he waited, the crowds formed below him under the tree. No one knew he was there. The murmuring of the crowd was closer. Nearer and nearer came Jesus, speaking to the people, touching some – he seemed like a man on fire.

And directly below the tree where Zacchaeus was, Jesus stopped. He looked straight up into the branches, into the frightened eyes of Zacchaeus, and said in a loud clear voice, 'Zacchaeus, come down out of that tree!'

The crowd became as silent as death. Little Zacchaeus clambered down and stood looking up at Jesus, the two of them surrounded by the huge crowd.

'Now the traitor will get his true desserts! Jesus will put him in his place.' Everyone waited.

'Tonight, Zacchaeus,' said Jesus clearly, 'I shall dine at your house.'

The eyes of Zacchaeus filled with tears. 'Sir, I will make everything ready.' And he ran off as fast as he could.

All of the people mumbled and grumbled and were bewildered.

'What was the great teacher doing, going to the house of a cheat, a swindler, a traitor to his own people, a ruthless hated man?'

And Jesus said to the mumblers and grumblers, 'Don't you see? I came to heal the lost, the swindlers and thieves and evil doers. People that are well do not need a doctor!'

And that night, in the house of Zacchaeus, there was another miracle. The heart of the little tax collector was healed and he could see with new, loving eyes.

'Jesus, sir,' he said, 'I will give half my belongings to the poor and I will pay back four times more to anyone I have cheated.'

From that day on Zacchaeus was a changed man. If he was still small, he had the biggest heart in Jericho. No one who asked him for help was ever refused.

But one little secret he kept to himself. Every day just before sunset, he would disappear. Little Zacchaeus crept quietly away from the house taking a bucket. He filled it at the well and then just before dark, thinking no one could see him, he made his way to the main street and there he watered the little sycamore tree that he climbed when he first saw Jesus.

17

Peter's Story: Dead and Alive

'The Son of Man must suffer much and be rejected by the elders,
the chief priests, and the teachers of the Law.
He will be put to death, but three days later he will be raised to life.'

~ LUKE 9: 22, GOOD NEWS BIBLE ~

NOO, it's when it gets roon tae the Passo'er – at this time o year –
that I mind on when Jesus died. Aye, we wir aw cast in a gloom as
black as nicht. We cudnae believe it. Jesus wis deid. The man we
thocht wis the Son o the livin God. The ane we thocht wid save Israel.
The ane we thocht wid free oor land o the Roman rule – aye, deid. I
jist sat doon, greetin like a bairn.

I cud mind no lang afore that – at Caesarea Philippi – Jesus turned
tae aw o us, an said, 'There's a wheen o talk gaun roon aboot wha I am.
Wha dae *ye* think I am?'

An I had this sort o flash – clear inspiration it wis – an afore ony yin
cud say a wurd, I said, 'Ye are the Son o God – the Messiah!' I e'en
tuik masel by surprise.

He luiked me straucht in the een, an cawd me 'Peter .... '

Usually I'd been kent as Simon, d'ye see, but he said, 'Peter ...
ye've spoken the truith. Ye *are* the rock, Peter.'

A rock? Weel, I wis a rock that wid crumble in the days tae come.

At that time, on the wey up tae the Passo'er in Jerusalem, Jesus wis aye speakin aboot hoo he wis gaun tae die. But, tae tell ye the truith, I didnae believe that in ma heart. Hoo cud the Son o God die? Efter aw, he'd done so mony amazin things raisin deid folk tae *life*. Naw, I didnae really believe him at the time. But it turned oot he wis richt and much worse than a nichtmare it wis – he wis betrayed by ane o us! For a few paltry pieces o silver, Judas, oor treisurer, sold him intae the haunds o his enemies. I wis in a fury. How cud Judas dae it? But I wisnae feelin awfy proud o masel either.

Ye see, it aw began wi sic a sense o promise, sic high hopes. Jesus ridin intae Jerusalem. Jesus wi palm leaves spread afore him – the sign o a king. An the crowd – all o us too – believed that Jesus wid miraculously rid oor country o the Roman army and gie us back oor ane land, oor ane government. Jesus, the Son o God, wid be oor king. It seemed as if we wir no jist at the Gates o Jerusalem, but at the gates o Paradise.

Whit a day that wis. An the supper in the upper room – all o us thegether – little thinkin it wis tae be oor last supper wi Jesus.

I mind he tuik the breid, an he blessed it an said, 'This is my body broken for you. Dae this in remembrance o me.'

It wis strange – nane o us kent whit he meant.

Then he said ane o us wid betray him. An that wis a hard notion tae swallow.

Efter supper we followed Jesus tae the Moont o Olives. Jesus stopped an turned tae us an said, 'This very nicht ye will ilk ane o ye desert me.'

We wir dumbfoonert. I said, 'Even if abody else deserts ye Lord, I never will.'

Jesus said, 'Peter, this very nicht, afore the cock crows, ye will disown me three times.'

'Oh, I wid die wi you afore I'd disown ye,' I said.

He jist luiked at me.

The rest o that weekend wis jist too terrible tae think aboot. Minutes later, his enemies arrested him in the garden. They got false witnesses at the trial, an they haunded him o'er tae the Romans.

Then Jesus wis forced tae cairry his ain cross through Jerusalem afore he wis hung up an crucified like a common criminal, atween twa reivers.

An whit Jesus said aboot me wis true, richt enough. For Jesus wis taen tae the hoose o Caiaphas for questionin. It wis a bitter cold nicht an I managed tae get intae the ootside courtyard, hopin tae get some news. I wis staundin roon the fire, tryin tae keep warm, when this servant lassie turned tae me in the glow o the flames an said, 'Are ye no ane o the followers o this Jesus?'

'No, I'm not! I dinna ken whit ye're talkin aboot,' I said, wi'oot thinkin.

Further intae the shadows, another o the lassies said, 'Hey, surely you wir wi this Jesus that they're questionin?'

An I cursed, an said, 'No! No! I dinna ken the man!'

Then there wis a bit o a pause an ane o the high priest's servants said, 'Ye've got the accent o a man o Galilee. Did I no see ye wi him in the olive grove where he wis arrested?'

An I fairly shouted at him, 'For God's sake! Did I no tell ye? I dinna ken the man!'

In the silence a cockerel crowed ... I found a corner an hid my face, because I cudnae hide the tears. Everythin had turned tae ashes. An noo Jesus wis gone, deid an buried in a tomb, covered ower by a great rock. An buried too were all oor hopes.

Whit cud we dae? Go back tae the fishin on the Sea o Galilee, where I first met Jesus an followed him wi'oot a second thocht? Left the fishin an everythin, an aw for whit? For this death?'

I mind Mary Magdalene, an Mary the mother o James, an some ither o the weemen folk, had prepared ointments tae pit on the body o Jesus. Ye see, he'd been buried jist afore the Sabbath an they wirnae allowed near him then. Thae weemen wir gaun tae go tae the tomb, but it wis guarded by Roman soldiers. They wanted tae see if they cud pit perfume an ointments on the body. I hadnae the heart tae go wi them. I watched them gaun – sad but brave.

I dinna ken hoo lang it wis, but suddenly they returned so excited we cud hardly make oot whit it wis they wir sayin.

'The rock! The big rock at the tomb! It wis rolled awa! Jesus wis gone! Twa men in white spoke tae them an said, "Why are you lookin for the livin amang the deid? He is risen. Do you no mind whit he told you?"' The women tumbled ower themsels in their eagerness tae tell the story.

Weel I didnae wait. I ran aw the wey tae the tomb tae find oot for masel. An whit dae ye think? It wis empty, richt enough – jist a few strips o cloth that had been rolled aboot the Lord's body an that wis aw – Jesus wis gone. That wis jist the beginnin. Funny thing, that death shud be the beginnin – but it wis, as ye'll hear.

Noo, we didnae richtly ken whit tae think, but we wir still feart that the same men that had done for Jesus wid get us tae, so we kept the doors locked.

Then suddenly, like oot o thin air, Jesus wis amang us again. An he showed us the very marks o the nails where he'd been crucified, for we wirnae awfy sure o him.

Thomas wisnae there that time an he didnae believe us. But, in the same way, Jesus appeared tae him an showed him his haunds. Thomas fell at his feet an said tae Jesus, 'Ma Lord an ma God!' – an he cudnae but believe. Seein wis believin wi Thomas.

After this, we went back tae Galilee. The weemen said that this wis the instruction o Jesus. Tae be quite truithful, I wis glad tae shake the dust o Jerusalem aff my feet.

Noo a strange thing happened when we wir back at the fishin. Things jist wirnae gaun weel. The nets wir empty. Then a man on the shore cried oot tae us, sayin, 'Cast on the ither side.'

An we did. Like a miracle, the net wis fu o fish. When we hauled the fish tae the shore, the man says, 'Bring some fish here.' An suddenly, we saw it wis Jesus again, alive here in Galilee.

He cooked the fish an we waited. Naebody spoke. Then he says, 'Come an eat' – an he broke the breid, jist like the last supper, the nicht afore he died.

Then he says tae me, 'Peter, do ye truly love me more than any ither?'

'Aye, Lord,' I said, 'ye ken I love you.'

'Feed my lambs,' he said.

An again he said tae me, 'Peter, son o John, do ye truly love me?'

An again I said, 'Aye, Lord, ye ken I love you.'

'Feed my sheep,' he said.

An a third time, he said, 'Peter, do ye love me?'

An I wis wonderin if mebbe he wis thinkin aboot the times I'd said I didnae ken him … but I said, an I cud feel the tears ahint my een, 'Aye, Lord, ye ken aw things an ye ken I love you.'

An again, he said, 'Feed my lambs.'

Noo that wis the third an last time that he appeared in the flesh, but he promised his spirit wid return an live inside us, jist as if he wir always alive. An that's what happened.

No lang efter this, we wir aw in Jerusalem an still feart o what micht happen tae us, when somethin like a flame seemed tae pour intae us. It wis the promise o Jesus tae come back like a livin spirit inside us. From that moment, fear left us an we spoke openly o the great Jesus Christ, an we prayed an preached on the very steps o the Temple.

We healed the sick in the name o Jesus, an some o us died for Jesus, but in a wey, like Jesus, they lived on. I know that, in thoosands o years, Jesus, in lands unknown tae me, among people unknown tae me, will live on ... an his love will move like a beautiful white dove o peace ower the hail world ... lang, lang efter I've gone from the earth tae join the king. I know too that I will never again deny him, even if I have tae die for him.

18

Jesus is Dead:
Pentecost:
The Great Commission

And there appeared to them
tongues like flames of fire,
dispersed among them and resting on each one.

~ ACTS 2: 3, NEW ENGLISH BIBLE ~

A LITTLE band of men and women huddled in a house in Jerusalem. What were they to think? They were confused; they were bewildered. They looked back at the strange, the terrible, the amazing events that had gripped their lives. They were followers of Jesus, the healer, the miracle worker, the Saviour of the world. They were remembering his amazing life, his terrible death, and his astonishing promises.

They could see, still so vividly, the day when darkness covered the sky, when the stones glistened like newly-scraped lead, and their faces were white with an eerie light under the cross where the son of God hung dying between two thieves, where their Jesus was dying.

And then, after three days, when their hearts broke, the miracle of miracles ... the rock was rolled from the tomb of Jesus and he returned from that land of death from which no traveller returns ... he returned and appeared in flesh and blood to Mary Magdalene and James' mother Mary, and later, again and again, to all of the disciples.

He had risen from the dead.

Not only had he risen from the dead, but he had spoken to them: 'Do not leave Jerusalem; wait for the gift I told you about, the gift my father promised. John baptised with water, but in a few days you will be baptised with the Holy Spirit.'

The Holy Spirit – what did *that* mean?

And then their Jesus had left them, risen as if drawn by a great shining light up into heaven, and they were left alone again.

Now they were in Jerusalem and they were waiting, but for what and for how long? Today the narrow streets of Jerusalem were crowded with people; it was the day of Pentecost, a Jewish Feast of the Harvest. From far and wide, from many lands, people had come to celebrate. The babble of many languages filled the air.

A sudden strange tremor ran through the followers of Jesus, and at the same moment there came a noise from the sky. It filled the whole house where they were sitting, and then what looked like tongues of fire spread from the sky and touched each one of the followers.

This is what Jesus had promised, this flame of the Holy Spirit. And at once they all rose fearlessly, like flames, and went outside where a large crowd had gathered to find the cause of this unearthly sound from the skies, this strange wind. And the sound began to fade as the followers, in loud voices, spoke about all the great things that God had done, and about Jesus, the Son of God, who had come to save them. Everyone was stunned and silenced because, of all that great band of people from many countries of the world, every single person heard the words in their own language.

'These people are drunk!' said a voice from the crowd. And others joined the chorus: 'Yes, these people are drunk! These people are drunk!'

Then Peter leapt on to a step of the Temple, with the other disciples around him, and said, 'No, no, my fellow Jews, these men are not drunk. It's only nine o'clock in the morning. No, this is what our Jesus promised; it is what your prophet Joel spoke about when he wrote: "God says, this is what I will do in the last days; I will pour out my spirit on everyone. Your sons and daughters will proclaim my message:

"Your young men will see visions
And your old men will have dreams.
I will perform miracles in the sky above
And wonders in the earth below.
There will be blood, fire and thick smoke;
The sun will be darkened,
and the moon will turn red as blood,
Before the great day of the Lord comes.
And then, whoever calls out to the Lord for help, will be saved."

'Listen, listen to my words, fellow Israelites,' said Peter. 'You all knew this man, Jesus of Nazareth. Through him God performed miracles and wonders and great healings among you. You could see that God was in him. And yet you killed him by letting sinful men crucify him. But God has raised this very Jesus from the dead! We have seen him *alive!* Thomas here has seen the very marks of the nails on his hands. This Jesus is now with his father in heaven and he has sent the power of his Holy Spirit into us. This is why we have a new power … this is why each of you understands us in your own language. Know this, you people of Israel – this Jesus, whom you crucified, is the one that God has made Messiah, the Promised One, the Saviour of the World. Believe this and be baptised in his name.'

Many people believed Peter's message – for that day about three thousand were baptised and became followers of Jesus.

The days that followed were among the strangest ever from the beginning of the world. These very first Christians, followers of Jesus, lived in a way that amazed everyone. They sold their possessions and shared with one another everything they had. There was no one in the whole group who was in need. Some who owned fields or houses, sold them and brought the money to the disciples who distributed the money according to each person's need. It was as if they were all brothers and sisters. It was a wonderful time, a time full of wonders.

One afternoon, Peter and John went to the Temple. At the gate of the Temple, the gate called the Gate Beautiful, there was a crippled beggar man. Every day he was carried to the Temple because he could not walk. He begged Peter and John to give him something.

'Look at us,' said Peter, 'we have no money. But I give you what

I have. In the name of Jesus Christ of Nazareth, I order you to get up and walk.'

Then Peter took him by his right hand and helped him up. At once the man's feet and ankles became strong. He stood up ... he started to walk around ... he jumped and yelled and shouted praise to the Lord, to Jesus of Nazareth in whose name he could walk and jump and run. Everyone who had known this poor beggar man for years was astonished and the whole town was full of talk of this new miracle brought about by the followers of Jesus of Nazareth.

But the leaders of the Jewish religion were not pleased. All this talk of a man risen from the dead, of this Jesus being the Son of God, was blasphemy to them and went against their deepest beliefs.

They were enraged to see the people in such large numbers follow- ing this new religion. So they had the guards of the Temple arrest Peter and John and throw them into jail. The next day Peter and John were made to stand before the court of the Temple priests. Then the High Priest said to them, 'By what power and in whose name do you do these things?'

Without hesitation, Peter answered, 'By the power of the Holy Spirit and in the name of Jesus Christ of Nazareth, whom you delivered to be crucified. By that power we healed the lame man.'

The High Priest and all the Jewish leaders were furious, but they knew that everyone in Jerusalem had heard about the curing of the beggar man. So they whispered amongst themselves and then said: 'You are forbidden, from now on, to speak or teach in the name of the man Jesus.'

Peter and John replied, 'Ask yourselves what is right: to obey you, or to obey God and what we have seen and know to be true.'

The High Priest warned them again, but he could do nothing be- cause the people were all praising God for what had happened – and the beggar man who had been healed was standing there right beside Peter and John, living proof of the power of their Christ.

All this was at the time of Pentecost, the coming of the Holy Spirit of God, a wind that was to blow the name of Jesus into the hearts and lives of men and women all over the world and into ages unborn.

King of Clowns

'People will come from the east and the west, from the north and the south,
and sit down at the feast in the Kingdom of God.
Then those who are now last will be first,
and those who are now first will be last.'

~ Luke 13: 29 - 30, Good News Bible ~

A BABY called David was born to be a king, but, strangely enough, from the earliest days he wanted to be not a king at all, but, of all things, a clown. His father, the King, and his mother, the Queen, used to laugh at him, but even when he was just a little fair-haired prince, he loved nothing better than the stories and tricks and jokes and patchwork clothes of the court jester.

Often he sat on the jester's knee. The jester would say, 'Your Highness ... or rather, your *Low*ness,' for the prince was very small at that time, 'your Royal Lowness ... when you become a Royal Highness, what would you like, with all your heart, to do?'

'With all my heart, ' cried the Prince, 'I would like to be a clown, a jester, a dancer, a juggler, and wear glittering clothes just like you, Diamond. [I forgot to mention, the court jester was called Diamond because of his glittering clothes, and his glittering dancing feet and his clever glittering words.]

'But my dear little Prince, you are to become a *king*, not a clown.'

'Well, I would like to be the *King* of Clowns,' said the Prince.

'King of Clowns, indeed,' said Diamond. 'I don't know if even a king is clever enough to become the King of Clowns.'

'I could learn to juggle and dance and sing and tell jokes, and .... '

'Oh ho, oh ho, oh ho, your Royal Lowness, that's only the very beginning. Listen to me, my Prince. Anyone can learn to juggle and dance and sing and tell jokes. Even an ordinary clown has to know much more ... *much* more ... and to be a *King* of Clowns ... well!'

'*What* more! *What* more! I will learn *everything* ... what *else* is there to learn?'

'The first thing you have to learn is that you are lower than everyone else in the world.'

'Then I'll keep the title you gave me. I'll call myself, "Your Lowness".'

Diamond laughed. 'Keep it in your heart, my Prince. Keep it in your heart.'

'What *else*? What *else* must I learn?'

'You must also learn to look straight into the hearts of people and straight into their thoughts, and you must love them so much that you want them to be happy .... '

'Even if their hearts are black and their thoughts are bad?'

'Yes, my Prince, *especially* if their hearts are black and their thoughts are bad.'

'Well,' said the little Prince, 'I will learn to do *all* these things.'

And suddenly the little Prince kneeled down before Diamond and said, 'Will you, Clown Diamond, be my teacher ... please?'

Diamond was so surprised and happy that a glittering tear ran down his clown's face, a tear as bright as any diamond, and he answered the Prince, 'Your Lowness ... Prince David ... it will be an honour.'

'Then why do you cry?' said the Prince.

'Because, my Prince, you must learn that sadness and happiness live together like brother and sister. Where one is, the other is never far away. It is the work of the clown to know the time to bring sadness and the time to bring happiness, the time to bring tears and the time to bring laughter.'

So when the diamond tear fell on the floor – a little clear drop – Diamond the Clown burst into a river of laughter. 'Yes, yes, yes, yes,

yes, yes, yes,' he cried, 'one day you will be clowned king!' and they both laughed. 'Yes, *truly* we will make you the greatest Clown King that ever there was.'

So he did. And this was a secret that only the Prince and the jester shared. It was a secret that they kept and shared right up till the day Diamond the jester grew old and died.

At length the old king also died. The Prince David, now a young man, became his Royal *High*ness, but in his secret heart he always called himself Your Lowness, as Diamond the jester had taught him. Indeed, that is how he became such a clever king who could look into the hearts of his people.

Often unknown to anyone, he would disguise himself as a ragged gypsy singer and move about among his people in the market-place, getting to know them; sometimes even in their homes, he would sing songs and exchange stories.

Now in the king's palace at that time, there was a young man. He was clever and handsome and had a silver tongue. Very quickly he became an important person – the Royal Entertainments Minister. It was his business to find musicians and actors and singers and dancers and to provide the palace entertainment on great occasions. His name, strangely enough, was also David, but he liked to be known by his full title – Chief Master of Royal Entertainments.

He ordered a splendid, flowing, golden cloak to be made for him, so that when he swished about the palace and the streets, he looked just like a king himself. In his heart he would like to have been the king. His father and mother were very lowly people, however, and he didn't like to visit them now because he was ashamed of their little cottage and ragged clothes.

On the day of his mother's birthday – she was now old and weak and sick – he decided this time he must visit her, but he waited until dark before making his way alone through the empty streets hoping to meet no one. Yet, he could not resist wearing his wonderful cloak.

When he arrived at his parents' little house, a surprise waited for him. He heard singing. He opened the door – sitting at the table, with a little cake and one candle, was his old father and mother ... *laughing!* ... for a ragged figure sat on a stool at the fireside playing a merry tune on the fiddle, merry and full of happiness.

'Oh, we thought you'd forgotten,' said his mother, 'but this gypsy man has given me a lovely birthday surprise. Welcome home, son. My, my, you *do* look grand.'

But David, the Chief Master of Royal Entertainments, was angry and jealous that this ragged gypsy should be at *his* fireside, celebrating *his* mother's birthday ....

Just then the gypsy man began to sing and dance:

'Oh, I am but a ragged thing
A raggle taggle ting ting ting
My cloak is made of the golden wind
And I tramp the road like a king, a king.'

And as he danced, David grew more and more angry, for the gypsy danced as if *he* wore a cloak of gold ....

David snatched the fiddle and broke it over the gypsy's face, shouting wildly, 'Leave this house and never come back!' He kicked the gypsy into the dark and slammed the door behind him. His mother blew out the candle to hide her tears.

At the palace the very next day, there was a great masked ball to celebrate the birthday of the old queen. The Chief Master of Royal Entertainments had excelled himself. The hall was bright with glittering crystal candles. Curtains of red and gold and blue hung from the pillars. It was beautiful and the very best musicians in the land made the music. The ladies wore silken gowns and the courtiers their finest tunics. Everyone wore a mask.

Just as the ball was reaching its height, the music stopped with a crash. There was silence. Into the middle of the great hall walked a figure wearing the mask of a clown. Without a word the figure approached the Chief Master of Royal Entertainments – who was easily recognised by his cloak of gold – and took him by the hand into the middle of the hall. Before all the people, he said, 'I wish to thank this man for making the best celebration in the world for my mother's birthday.'

And the clown took off his mask. It was King David. One side of his face was black and blue, bruised all the colours of a rainbow.

At once the Chief Master of Royal Entertainments realised that this was the gypsy from his mother's house, the king himself. He went pale with fear.

'Why are you staring?' asked the king. Indeed, *everyone* was staring at the king by that time.

'Your *f..., f..., face!*' stammered his Master of Entertainments.

'Oh, yes!' said the king. 'Would you believe it? Some rogue hit me over the head with my own fiddle.'

'Have him whipped,' said a courtier.

'Have him banished,' said another.

'Have him hanged,' said a third.

'And what would *you* do with such a person?' King David asked his namesake, the Master of Entertainments.

'I ... I don't know, your majesty,' stuttered the Master of Entertainments, 'I'm sure he deserves to be *severely* punished.'

'Take off your mask,' said the king.

The Master of Entertainments was faint with fear. Would he be whipped? Would he be banished? Would he be hanged? At the least he would be the most unpopular man in the kingdom.

'Your mask,' repeated King David.

No sooner had the Master of Entertainments removed it than the young king strode up, looked at him closely, then said, 'The moment we have been waiting for!' He raised his hand – twelve trumpeters blew a loud fanfare and great crimson curtains opened at the end of the hall to reveal a huge banquet table. Sitting at it were two women dressed in fine robes.

'Here,' commanded the king of his Master of Entertainments, 'take these gifts to the highest table. Sitting there are the two queens of our lives – your mother and my mother. They are the guests of honour tonight.' And the king hugged his Master of Entertainments and whispered in his ear something that no one heard.

The Master of Entertainments staggered back and nearly toppled over. He fell low on his knees and whispered, 'How can I thank you, your Majesty?' No one but the king knew what he meant.

'I'm sure you'll find a way,' said the king quietly.

That night the king had a dream. He dreamt he was a little boy again and that his old friend Diamond the jester sat him on his knee and said, 'Oh ho, oh ho, oh ho, your Royal Lowness, you are learning, you are learning, you are learning. Soon you will truly be a King of Clowns. I've been watching you from my glittering home among the stars in the skies. I'm proud of you, my little prince, and I see you have an apprentice.'

'An apprentice?' asked the king.

'You will see, you will see,' said the old jester and disappeared in a cloud of laughter and diamonds.

When the king awoke, a little glittering tear ran down his face.

Well, his dream did not puzzle him for long. When he went to visit his mother that day, he paused at her door, for he heard her bubbling with laughter.

'You look so funny!' she cried. The king opened the door and looked in. Who should be with the old queen but the Chief Master of Royal Entertainments wearing not a golden cloak, but a baggy suit and the painted face of a clown. The king smiled, closed the door quietly, and as he left he was sure he heard the unmistakable laughter of the old jester Diamond.

The Prince
and the Tramp

Where your treasure is,
there your heart will be also.

~ LUKE 12: 24, NEW REVISED STANDARD VERSION ~

I'M going to tell you about a great kingdom, a kingdom of beautiful trees, fresh, clear, tumbling rivers, bright blue skies and a smiling people with sparkling eyes. The king and his queen ruled over people that were very content with what they had, and often did the king walk unrecognised amongst his subjects just to see how they fared.

This country was famous for its hospitality. It was said by travellers that the doors of its people were always open to a passing stranger. Indeed, above the main door of the Royal Palace itself, stood in big letters carved in wood the word *'Eenyalcom'*, which, in the language of that country, meant 'You are all welcome.'

But not only were doors always open, but the people were great visitors. They were *always* visiting each other. Often, during these visits, someone would tell a story, another sing a song, yet another bring out a fiddle – in no time at all, there would be dancing and merry-making till the moon was high in the dark blue sky.

And, under the silver light of the moon, chattering and sometimes still singing, the people would walk home – for they were also great walkers, the people of that country. In fact, they were nearly as famous for walking great distances as they were for their great hospitality. It was a delightful country to visit and you were always welcome.

But all this was in the good old days. For a disease had fallen on the people. Now there was little storytelling or singing or dancing or playing the fiddle, or walking home arm in arm under the kind light of the silver moon. Even the skies had turned grey. Few people walked anywhere, but retired behind locked doors, and sat in darkened rooms, staring at flickering pictures on the walls. The doors were no longer open to passing strangers; travellers no longer felt welcome. Even the letters on the sign above the Royal Palace were covered with a green mould – you could no longer read the word that meant 'Welcome'.

You could see a letter 'E', the top part of the 'Y', and an 'L'. One old villager said it now looked like the word in their language for 'Evil'. Whether that is true or not, it looked foosty and ugly and un-welcoming.

You might wonder how it happened that such a lovely place should become so ugly and diseased. It happened in a quite unexpected way. It happened because the old king listened to a visitor who promised him happiness beyond his wildest dreams. Here is what happened.

A tall, thin man, with a clever unsmiling face, came one day to the palace. 'I am an ambassador of great news, your High Majesty. Great news, your most High, Mighty and Adored Majesty,' said the tall stranger.

'I wish he wouldn't use so many words,' muttered the queen. 'Too many words!'

'I know you wish your simply superb subjects to be super, super, super happy,' continued the visitor.

'Too many words,' muttered the queen.

'I can, you see,' continued the stranger, 'supply you with the universal secret of universal happiness. You ... em ... *do* wish your subjects to be happy, your Exalted Highness?'

'Yes! yes!' agreed the king.

'Then leave it in my hands. I will arrange for them to be protected; they will be safe as houses and happy. All I need at first is a few blacksmiths, for I have heard that a thief has entered your kingdom and that he may steal even from this palace at any moment. Even now,' he whispered in the king's ear, 'he may be stealing the richest thing in the palace. But, don't worry, I will get you the key to happiness.'

He got the king a huge key, and the huge key was fitted to the palace gates so that the king could feel safe and happy again. Keys and locks were on sale everywhere – bigger and better and safer and more expensive. For added protection, a good business in sharp knives was started up.

One day the king said to this stranger, 'My people will surely be lonely now that they're all locked into their houses. They don't walk about and visit and talk with each other any more.'

'Aha, indeed, your Glorious High Majesty,' said the stranger in his dark suit – just so. You are the wisest of monarchs, the cleverest of kings.'

'Too many words,' murmured the queen.

'Indeed, indeed,' continued the stranger. 'Now that your subjects are safe, safely locked in their houses, safe from thieves, I can sell you a magic machine that will tell them stories in pictures and they will not need to walk out or about at all. They will be safe and happy. They will not even need friends. It will be money well spent.'

'But they can't talk to a machine!' muttered the queen.

'Money well spent. They will be safe and happy,' purred the honey-lipped stranger.

But, at the same time, the disease came. Many of the older people just stopped breathing. For some, their hearts just stopped beating for no visible reason and no doctor in the place could find a cure. Even experts from abroad were baffled.

Then one day a tramp strolled into town with his ragged little dog, a penny whistle, and very little else ....

He had nothing, but he didn't seem to have a care in the world either. He sat down amongst a few of the drunks in the market-place and began to play his whistle. The notes danced in the air and his ragged dog, with its bright eyes, wagged its tail. One of the drunks woke up. 'Reminds me of the old days,' he said, 'the *good* old days. You should get out of here,' the drunk advised, 'get out while ye've still got a tune in you. This place has got the kiss of death. It's doomed.'

97

'But I thought this place was famous for its welcome and singing and dancing and merry-making and laughter,' said the tramp.

'Laughter? What's *laughter?*' roared the drunk. 'I've forgotten the sound of laughter. No, this place is famous for keys and locks and knives and minding your own business and drinking and dying .... The whole kingdom's been sick ever since yon dark stranger promised the old king the earth and the daft gowk believed him. I'm afraid you're out of date, pal.'

'I must have a word with this king,' said the tramp.

'Well, you'll need a *huge* key!' The drunk laughed for the first time in years, rolled over and fell fast asleep in the gutter where Ruggles, the tramp's dog, gave his face a friendly lick. The drunk snored peacefully on with a smile on his face.

The palace gate was indeed locked. The tramp began to play his penny whistle. Dazzling jigs, strathspeys, reels and fairy dances ... and soon a crowd of citizens gathered round. At length, as if by magic, there was a great creaking and the palace gates opened. The king himself appeared. He was now an old and bent and weak man. This was the first time the people had seen him in years.

'Aha, a fine tune,' he said. 'I remember it well. It reminds me of the old days, the *good* old days.'

Many of the old subjects sighed.

'Mmm,' said the king, 'I would give my whole kingdom to cure my land of this terrible disease, my *whole* kingdom.'

The tramp stopped playing his whistle. 'Sir,' he said, 'I will cure your kingdom.' At that, the whole crowd – led by the drunk from the square – hooted with a laughter as sharp as daggers and as cruel as knives. The tramp turned and, with his little dog, began to walk slowly away, the dog with its tail proudly in the air.

'Oh *wait* ... please wait. Could you really find a cure?' It was Karl, the king's son, who asked.

'Aye,' said the tramp, 'I *know* the cure. But what would you give for it?'

'I would give you *anything* in the world for it,' said the young prince. '*Anything.*'

'Aye, well, we'll see,' said the tramp. 'In that case, follow me and I'll show you.'

And he began to walk away, playing the penny whistle. To everyone's astonishment, the three of them – Ruggles, the tramp and the prince – disappeared without a word into the gloaming.

And that was the last that was heard of the prince for a very long time – of the prince, the tramp, or of Ruggles!

Nothing improved in the kingdom. If anything, things grew worse. The people were idle, as if they suffered a kind of sleeping sickness. What energy they had, they used to make sure no thief entered their houses. Little did they know that the 'thief' had his *own* key.

And in the palace, the king and queen sat lonely behind the great locked door, without the apple of their eyes, their son Karl. The years passed slowly – Spring, Summer, Autumn, Winter – for several cycles.

Meanwhile, Karl, Ruggles and the tramp were busy on their journey.

'Where will we stay?' asked the prince on the first night.

'With the sparrows,' said the tramp. And that night the prince slept on a bed of leaves in the forest. And they needed no key, because there was no door.

'Where will we go now?' said the prince, when they wakened in the sun on the second day.

'I will play a tune, then we'll follow our noses,' said the tramp.

'When will we find the cure?' said the prince, when they woke up on the edge of another town on the third day.

'Maybe tomorrow,' said the tramp. 'You will find it on our journey, if you have eyes to see, ears to hear, and a heart to know.'

Ruggles wagged his tail.

And that is how they travelled – the tramp, the Prince and Ruggles, following their noses. But the prince kept the tramp's words in his heart. They worked a day here, a day there, earning just enough to live on. And always the prince watched this extraordinary, happy tramp. He seemed to be quite happy to help people for no more than a night's rest and a scrap of food, and sometimes for nothing more than a 'thank-you'.

They had journeyed for a year and a day when they came across an old man sitting hunched outside his cottage. Soldiers had looted his house and left him with nothing. 'I'll go and find him something to eat and drink,' said the prince.

The tramp smiled knowingly and played his whistle.

And still they journeyed onwards, until one very cold day they found a baby lying in the snow. 'I'll wrap him up in my cloak,' said the prince.

The tramp played his whistle, saying nothing.

The next day, the baby was sick and the prince found a hospital and a doctor. On that day, the prince began to whistle one of the tramp's tunes, and you could have sworn that Ruggles laughed, or maybe he just barked, in tune.

'A man is to be hanged,' said the tramp on another day. 'See, the black flag is waving above the prison.'

The tramp played a slow and sad tune on his whistle.

'Why that sad tune?' asked the Prince. 'The man must have done a desperate thing if he is to be executed.'

'Yes,' said the tramp. 'But I am sad that any man should come to such a sad place that he should kill one of his brothers.'

The prince paced up and down. At length, he said, 'I am going to the prison to visit that man.'

The tramp continued to play his sad tune. When the prince returned that evening, he was much changed. He had heard the story of the man who was now dead.

For seven years they travelled together like this, and at length they came to the prince's own country. And, one day in Spring, they came to the very palace of the king, his father.

By now the dark stranger held the post of Royal Chief of Security and Supplier of Picture Machines for the whole kingdom.

The tramp and Ruggles and the prince walked into the village. The street was empty … no sign of any people … the doors of all the houses locked. Finally they arrived at the gates of the palace, which were locked and bolted.

The king and queen sat in a large room with no windows. They were pale and frail and watched a huge machine with moving pictures. They did not speak to each other.

Suddenly the king sat up. 'Did I hear something? A dog barking? An old tune on a penny whistle?' he asked, perking up a bit.

'No, no, nothing,' said the dark stranger, who sat beside them like a jailer.

'Silence!' said the queen, hushing the stranger. 'I hear music, *real* music! *Living* music! Unlock the doors! Unlock the gates at once!'

'But your most Royal Highness ....'

'No more *words!*' thundered the queen in a voice that turned the stranger green with fear. 'Now open ... unlock ... *everything* ... this very minute ... now!' So the stranger took out a huge bunch of keys and unlocked door after door after door until they came to the great gate of the palace itself.

'Open it!' said the queen menacingly.

The door flew open. And there was the tramp playing his whistle, Ruggles barking and the prince dancing!

The prince ran into the arms of his mother and the old king clasped him with joy.

'Give me those keys!' the queen demanded of the dark stranger. She snatched them, then she threw them far out into the river where they sank without trace.

'If you do not leave this town immediately, and take your keys and locks and machines with you ... ' she shouted at the Royal Chief of Security and Supplier of Picture Machines, 'you will follow these keys to the bottom of the river ... forever!'

The dark stranger scuttled off.

'Now, I'm going to have the *greatest* feast we have ever had in this kingdom,' said the frail old king gleefully. 'The whole kingdom is going to celebrate. My cherished son has returned. There is to be dancing and singing and fiddle-playing.'

The whole country did celebrate and all the doors of all the houses were unlocked and left ajar. Dusty fiddles were brought out and some songs were croaked and a few old tales told. The palace gates were thrown open. And no one noticed the dark stranger creeping out of the gates of the village, taking his own dark journey, looking for another town where he could sell the people padlocks and keys and fear and his clever machines.

In the great hall, there was joy and there was grief. That night the old king rose and gave a speech. 'My people,' he said, 'this is the cure. Now we are together again. Yes, this is the cure. This is worth my whole kingdom. It is the happiest moment of my life.'

And he sat down smiling and peacefully he sighed one last sigh before he died ....

His funeral was full of music and dancing, just as he would have wished. Everyone was glad that, after so many years of sadness, he had died a happy man surrounded by people he loved and his old beloved music.

After the funeral, the prince turned to the tramp and said, 'All these years I have travelled with you, looking for the cure – and now I see the cure is simple. You're not a tramp, are you? You are worthy to be our king. I will keep my father's promise and, from now on, there shall be but one key, the key of welcome to the kingdom – and it is yours.'

The tramp smiled, 'No, I have my journey to continue. You keep the key, you have earned it. Teach your people how to be tramps!'

He laughed. 'Come on, Ruggles,' he said. And he picked up his whistle and together they walked away out through the open palace gate, under a sky where a patch or two of blue could be seen.

And the dog barked at a little tree.

21

The Licht
o the Warld

'And every one who hears these words of mine and does not do them
will be like a foolish man who built his house upon the sand;
and the rain fell, and the floods came, and the winds blew
and beat against that house, and it fell ....'

~ MATTHEW 7: 26 - 27, REVISED STANDARD VERSION ~

MAYBE this story comes from the distant past, maybe from the far
future. Who knows? But it is, or was, or is to be, located in a time
when a mutant race of humankind – pale ghost-like creatures of men
and women (and children too) – inhabited a kingdom far, far underneath our earth. And the people – these gremlin-like creatures – had
brought great trouble upon themselves.

In this land of darkness, a fear descended upon the people when a
disease broke out amongst them. It was the most frightening of all
diseases, for they were losing their sight – going blind. And the richest
folk, the most powerful, they were affected worst of all. Everyone was
afraid. They could find no cure.

And so, at last, they went – a whole village – to visit the old and
wise storyteller. They gathered outside his cave.

He gazed back at them from his cave, deep in the earth. 'There
wis a time ... aye, there wis a time,' said the auld sennachie, the teller

103

of stories. 'Aye, there wis a time we didna bide here in the mirk o daurkness under the earth. Na, na, we bade in the braid licht o day under the gowden sun o the great God. Fowk were blythe then, fowk were merry; there was muckle dauncin an singin. Fowk didna lock an bolt their doors – for nane wid steal an nane wid dae ye ony hairm.'

In the firelight, the eyes of the old man glittered. Everyone in the village was gathered to hear the words of the storyteller. For years he had been silent, for years he had been ignored, for years people had forgotten his wisdom, forgotten the power of his inner eye, his power to see into the future. But now he stood at the mouth of his cave and they all huddled in a silent circle. For once, they listened to the fiery words of the old man. For now they were in trouble, deep trouble, and they didn't know where to turn.

'Aye, aye, ye broke an tint yin warld an noo ye'll brak anither!' The old man began to speak again. 'Aye, here we bide in the daurk ablow a hail warld ye brak. An ye brak the hert of the great God wha built it. Aye, here we bide in a kingdom o daurkness – but waur nor that ye bide in *inner* daurk, ye hae herts o daurkness.

> *Black as nicht*
> *Ye hae nae licht*
> *Ye hae nae licht.*

The eyes of the old man burned; his tongue was a fire. For a time he was silent ... for a *long* time. He raised a finger and pointed round the circle. 'Ye hae forgotten silence.'

But no one knew what the old man meant.

'Ye had a bonnie warld an ye made a bonnie mess o it. Ye blastit and wastit aw the bonnie trees, aw the rivers an seas, the caller air and the creatures o the seas an land. Ye wounded the minds o bairns wi ugsome sights. Ye tellt them tae want an want, an tak an tak, until they were eaten up wi a greed that swallowed this hail an bonnie earth. An noo that ye are a frichtit again, ye come tae me. Aye, noo that there's a disease amang ye, ye come tae me. Weel, I canna cure ye – ye'll hae tae cure yersels. I ken ye're gaun blin – ye canna see an ye're frichtit. An ye haud on tae things an bolt yer doors, for ye're feared ye winna see the thief.

'An ye winna see the thief! Ye winna see the thief, for he's stolen yer sense, an stolen awa the licht o kindness fae yer e'en. He's stolen the welcome fae yer herts and pit a cal ice o greed in its place. There wis a time when yer doors were open, when a'body wis welcome an there wisna a thief tae be seen. Noo yer doors are locked an ye canna see the thief. The thief will gang when ye unlock yer doors. Aye ye're gaun blin … an ye're frichtit … an ye canna see the thief.

'But … I'll tell ye yin thing, a bairn will lead ye tae the thief and a woman will bring the licht back tae yer een.'

With these words, the old man disappeared into the gloom of his cave and all the people returned to their homes and locked their doors and agreed that the old man was clearly mad. It had been a foolish idea to ask him to cure their sickness anyhow. After all, if doctors couldn't, how could he?

But as the days passed, the blindness among the people worsened – their sight was growing dim. It was getting more and more difficult for them to see each other. And they became more and more afraid that people could cheat them, steal from them, give them the wrong change, creep into their houses even – so laws against thieves became more and more strict. Finally it was decided that an example should be made of the next person to be caught stealing. The thief was to be expelled from the safety of the underground kingdom and thrown out into the empty earth above.

And that is how, as you will see, the forgotten words of the old man came to be true.

It happened that there was, in that underground village, a very poor woman who had a little boy who could see very well, but was so hungry that he could hardly walk. His mother, whose name was Amat, knew that unless he had food soon, the little boy would surely die.

So she knocked on the door of a house where, her nose told her, beautiful food was being cooked. The smell made tears of hunger cloud her own blue eyes.

She heard bolts being drawn back and keys being unlocked, and soon, before her, stood one of the roundest and richest and best judges in the village. He peered at her with shortsighted eyes.

'Eh, who are you? What do you want?'

'I am Amat, sir, a pair woman whas bairn is seek. All I want is a bit o food for the lad. He's seek, sir, but he has sic bonnie e'en that can see in the daurk. I dinna want him to die.'

'Well, neither do I,' said the fat judge. 'Where is he?'

'Here, sir, beside me.'

'His name?'

'Visu, sir.'

'Good, I will keep him, and he will be my eyes. Here is a loaf of bread for you. I will take your son.'

'Oh, but sir, ye canna tak my bairn! Ye canna!'

'I will have him for my eyes. Take your bread and go!'

'Thief! Thief! Thief!' shouted Visu loudly. 'Thief! Thief!' He did not want to be separated from his mother.

At once people rushed from all directions towards the house of the judge.

'There!' roared the judge, pointing at Amat. 'Over there – see, she has stolen my loaf! Take her to prison.'

The people, of course, believed *him.* After all, wasn't he a judge? And there she was clutching the loaf in her arms.

And so it was that, although no one realised it, the first part of the storyteller's prophecy came true: a bairn would find the thief.

Poor Amat was tried and found guilty. As a punishment, she was banished, expelled, from the underground kingdom and thrust out into the world above.

So she was led onwards, upwards through caves and passages until finally a huge boulder was levered aside and she was thrown out into the strange world above. The boulder thudded back into place and Amat could see nothing for the brightness of the sun. She wept. She was alone. Her son had been stolen from her. Amat had been branded a thief and she did not know where she was.

But as she lay on the ground, through her tears she saw a shape ... surrounded by stars ... and a soft voice, the voice of a woman, spoke to her. And the voice spoke in the same tongue as the old sennachie, the storyteller. 'Dinna be feart, lassie ... dinna be feart. Ye can hae food an shelter an a place tae lay yer heid. When ye're rested, ye can tell yer story. I hae gran lugs tae hear wi.'

Amat fell asleep. In the morning, when her eyes became accustomed to the light, she saw that she was surrounded by people with glowing smiling faces. They seemed to be filled with light and it seemed to her that these people of the upper earth must be angels. So she told them her story.

They found it hard to believe that anyone of the under earth could be so cruel and tell such lies – especially a judge. They listened closely to her story – about the blindness of all the people ... and about their terrible fear.

Then the woman, who first found Amat beside the great boulder, said: 'My sister, for we are aw brithers an sisters, ye ken – ye maun tak the Licht back intil that land o blindness fae whaur ye cam. An first, ye maun tak it to the judge, yer muckle fat brither.'

And Dea, for that was the woman's name, gave Amat the secret of Light and they returned to the great rock, the shape of a huge bird's egg, where Amat had emerged from the land of darkness.

As if by magic, Dea rolled back the great rock, kissed her sister Amat lightly on the forehead, saying, 'Dinna be feart an a sall be weel.'

Amat thanked her sister. And the rock closed behind her.

Now, when Amat returned to the land of the underworld folk, she was glowing with Light. She was not afraid – and her sight was perfect, for she knew the secret of Light.

First of all, she went to the house of the fat judge. He was now almost totally blind and used Amat's son as a guide-child, just like a guide-dog. A great crowd was there, for it was the judge's birthday.

Into the room walked Amat, beautiful and glowing with Light. Everyone fell silent. No one knew who this beautiful woman was – except Visu her son who waited silently to see what his beautiful lost mother would say.

Well, she walked straight up to the judge. Dimly, dimly through his misted eyes he began to see the Light.

Amat said: 'Ye pair blin cratur, I forgie ye. Dinna be feart.'

An at once, the judge recognised the voice. He fell down on his knees and, before all the people, cried out, 'I am a thief! I stole this good woman's son! And I am a liar, for I blamed her! I deserve to be thrown out of this kingdom into the empty earth above.'

'Ah weel,' said Amat, 'I see that ye can see the truth a wee bittie.'

And at that minute a miracle happened.

'Oh, I *can*!' said the judge, 'I *can* see the truth and I can see you – oh, praise be to God, I can *see*!'

So that was how the Light of the World came to the underworld, and how the prophecy of the old sennachie came to be true that 'a bairn will lead ye tae the thief and a woman will bring the licht back tae yer e'en.'

The days of dancing and singing, visiting and storytelling, returned to the village of the underworld. Over and over they tell the story of the judge who was blind and saw, the respected judge who confessed to being a thief. They talk of the storyteller and his prophecy. All of this keeps the light of the world dancing in their eyes and their hearts.

And at the gate of their village is a sign that says, 'BROTHERS AND SISTERS, YOU ARE *ALL* WELCOME'.

Sometimes, of course, they get a little shortsighted and forget – because after all, like you and me, they are not perfect ....

STORIES OF TODAY

22

The Key
to Happiness

I don't care if you're red or green,
purple or pink or blue;
The person I love lives inside
the friend that I call, 'You'.

~ RAINBOW FRIEND *by* LINDA BANDELIER ~

JULIA lived in the biggest house in the village – or *nearly* in the village.
It stood, Julia's house, just outside the village in its own grounds,
behind tall stone walls.

Morag lived in a tumble-down cottage by the river in the original
part of the village. The cottage was long and low and old – it had a
tangled backyard that led to a rickety hut hanging perilously over
the river. To the surprise of a number of people, Julia and Morag were
the best of best friends.

Julia had silky fair hair. Her eyes were sky blue. But, for most of the
time, she seemed sombre and even sad, except when she was with her
friend Morag. Morag's dark eyes would glitter like a gypsy's when she
told Julia stories of her terrible uncle who came home from the sea
with tales that could freeze your blood or make you lie on the floor
kicking your legs with laughter. Julia loved to be told these stories.

It was the beginning of a lovely autumn, but for once it was Morag

109

who seemed to be under a cloud. In fact, she was plain down-in-the-dumps fed-up. 'Seek at hairt,' as her granny would say.

You see, it would soon be Julia's birthday and Julia was going to have a big party and invite lots of people Morag didn't know. They would wear lovely dresses and give Julia beautiful presents. Celia Landford, for instance, would give Julia the most expensive birthday present she had ever bought anyone ever, ever. Morag didn't like Celia, who was clever and pale and had eyes like a weasel – or so Morag thought.

Morag had no money and she didn't know how she could get a present for Julia and so she was 'hairt seek' fed-up, down-in-the-dumps.

The hut at the foot of Morag's backyard was her most secret and favourite place. She was sitting there now, but for once all its treasures failed to cheer her up. She looked at herself in the cobwebby old mirror and saw a sad face looking back at her with dark eyes.

'Well, what are you going to do, glumfy face?' asked her reflection.

'I'm going to say I'm sick and just not go!' she replied.

'Oh that's great, glumfy face, be a real wee coward!' said her other self.

'Stop calling me glumfy face ... and anyhow, what can I give Julia as a present? Nothing will be half so good as *Celia's* present.'

Morag turned away from the glum face in the mirror and looked at the rubble and junk all around her and picked out a dusty old book. It was a book of fairy tales. It fell open at the story of Cinderella ....

'You know, she's just like me,' thought Morag, 'no money, and wanting to go to the ball.' When she finished reading the story, she had an idea. It turned out, as you'll see, not to be a very good idea. In fact, it turned out to be almost a *disastrous* idea.

Morag's idea was this: she would play the fairy godmother and bring her friend Julia the *best* present in the world. She would bring her a better present than anyone else, better by far than any present Celia Landford could ever dream of .... This was how she was going to do it: she would stop eating dinner and save up all her school dinner money. Then she would buy ... she would buy ... well, she would think of that later, but it would be the *very best* that money could buy.

So Morag glared at herself in the mirror through the cobwebs and said, 'So there!' But although she did not know it, that was when her real troubles began. She took the large key out of her purse, locked the door of the hut and strode through the tangled trees home to the long, low cottage.

'Shall we play shops today in the hut?' asked Morag's two little brothers. 'Please?'

'No, no, not today,' said Morag, 'not today.'

It was three weeks later. The trees were red and yellow and brown. Leaves were beginning to fall. Julia and Morag were having a walk together. Morag was hungry. Cold winds made her shiver and her eyes had lost some of their brightness.

'Tell me more about your secret hut,' said Julia. 'Tell me about the games you play in it. Tell me the stories your uncle tells when he sits in the hut that leans over the river. When he calls out *Land Ahoy!* in a loud Captain's voice and tells you all about the cannibals and the jungles. Tell me, Morag .... '

But Morag was somewhere else: she was rehearsing the moment when she would be the fairy godmother with the best present in the world.

'Morag! Morag!' pleaded Julia. '*Tell* me .... '

'Och no, not just now! Not now!' Morag snapped at her friend and they walked on silently through the village street.

As they passed the village shop, just to break the ice, Julia pointed at a gold box in the window and said, 'Those are my favourite chocolates.' Morag stored the information in her mind, like a squirrel.

The trees were growing barer. Morag went to the hut every day now. Not as before, with her brothers, to play. Not even when her uncle visited, with his red cheeks and loud voice and offer of stories from the ship's bridge of the hut's window overlooking the river. No, now she went to the hut to take each day's dinner money and add it to her secret store in the box hidden under the book of fairy tales with Cinderella in it. Every day she thought of being the fairy godmother, but every day she was growing thinner and paler and snappier. And she always remembered to lock the door carefully.

'Thon lassie's no lookin at all weel,' said her uncle.

'Aye, she looks hairt-seek,' said her granny.

But all ready beside the moneybox with its pound notes there was a golden box of chocolates. The chocolates were just the first present. She was still looking for the best present that money could buy. And every day she looked in the shops, she read the mail-order magazines, she watched all the advertisements on television – while growing thinner and thinner, until her large brown eyes were huge in her pale face.

The birthday party was getting nearer and still she hadn't found just exactly the right present.

One day, Julia said to her, 'There is one thing I'd really like for my birthday.'

'What's that?' asked Morag.

'I can't tell you,' said Julia, 'but it would be the best present ever. It would be like a key to happiness.'

This just made Morag more worried. What could it be? Would weasily Celia know what it was and give it to Julia?

'Tell me,' said Julia, 'why don't you ever tell me about your secret hut any more, and the games you play with your brothers, and your uncle's stories and visits? I'd love to hear one of your uncle's stories.'

'We don't play games now. We don't have stories.'

'Why not?'

But Morag did not say. Julia was doing her best. Morag was her only real friend, but she seemed to be losing her. It was as if, as the nights grew darker, a curse was falling upon Morag. She was becoming thin and so silent, as if she was bewitched and pining away.

Poor Julia was even more lonely than ever in her big house. Now, when she came to school and to the village, she was met by those large, brown, sad eyes. Julia thought to herself, 'It's as if Morag is becoming as lonely and sad as me.'

Now the day of Julia's party was just one week away. Five day's dinner money to go. Through the cobwebs, out of the mirror, a face she could hardly recognise looked at Morag. It was the face of a thin, pinched creature, like a weasel. The eyes glittered in the gaunt cheeks.

'So what present are you going to buy?' whispered her reflection in a voice as fragile as glass.

'Och, I'll wait till the last minute,' she replied.

'And then what?' hissed the ghastly reflection.

'And then I'll buy the *best* present money can buy.'

'We'll see,' said the ghostly face. It seemed to smile a wicked smile.

Quickly, Morag counted the pound notes. Twenty-eight, twenty-nine, thirty ... wow, a fortune!

Although Morag's stomach was sore and she felt weak, she would buy an *unbelievable* present.

That week a storm blew nearly all the leaves from the trees. Morag had terrible dreams every night. She couldn't think clearly.

'Tell me whit's wrang wi' ye, lass?' said her Granny, gently, in the morning. 'Whit's happened tae yer cherry blether the day?'

Morag had nothing to say. The party was on Saturday. It was to begin at three o'clock. All the shops in the village closed for a half day on Saturday at one o'clock prompt.

But at half past one, Morag was sitting alone in the hut at the foot of her backyard. As she looked out, a last brown leaf fluttered to the ground. She had failed. She had failed to get a present. She lifted up the dusty fairy book, she took up the money box and opened it. Thirty five pounds! At least she had the golden box with the chocolates in it. What did they look like? She would take a peek inside. She carefully opened the box and oh … those lovely shapes … hearts and diamonds and little dimpled balls filled with strawberries. She was aching with hunger. She would eat just one. It was delicious.

She ate every single chocolate ….

Aghast, Morag caught sight of her guilty, frightened face in the mirror. Now she had no present at all. Only the thirty five pounds.

But then she remembered what Julia had said to her. 'There is one thing I'd really like for my birthday … it would be the best present ever. It would be like a key to happiness.'

Suddenly Morag was struck, as if by lightning. Well, that was it! She would give Julia all the money – the thirty-five pounds – and Julia could buy her heart's desire, her very own key to happiness. That was it. Money was the best present money could buy. So, she put all the money into the golden chocolate box. That would be the biggest surprise at the party.

Morag arrived late to the party at the big house. Everyone was sitting down at the big oval table. Celia sat beside Julia, chattering. Morag was feeling sick, her stomach fluttering, her mouth dry.

Julia jumped up when she saw her friend. 'Ah, Morag – how lovely, how lovely to see you!'

'Here,' said Morag, and she handed her friend Julia the golden chocolate box.

'How lovely! My favourite chocolates! What a nice present. I'll open them as soon as we finish eating. Come on, squeeze in here beside me.'

But by the time the birthday feast was finished, Morag felt completely ill with all the excitement, the chocolates and the rich food.

'Now,' said Julia, 'we'll have Morag's chocolates.'

'It's ... eh ... not chocolates,' Morag stammered. There was silence. 'It's my present for you.'

Julia opened the chocolate box. In the hush, everyone waited to see what was inside. Julia looked puzzled.

Celia suddenly jumped up and laughed. 'That's not a present! That's money!'

The pound notes fluttered to the floor like tired leaves. Everyone burst out laughing. 'That's not a present! It's money!'

Morag ran from the house, followed by the gales of laughter. She fled to the dark woods and sat cold and alone and sick at heart.

All that week, she lay ill in bed with a fever. When the doctor allowed her to have visitors, Julia came to see her.

At first, not one of them spoke. And then Julia said, 'I've brought your present back. My parents told me I had to.'

It was still in the golden chocolate box.

Morag looked at the box. 'But I wanted you to buy whatever you wanted. I wanted you to get the best present you could ever have ... like that key to happiness.'

'But that's not what I meant,' said Julia. 'That's not what I meant at all. I was just thinking of ... the key to your secret hut. I wanted you to invite me in to play with you ... that's all.

Eric Liddell

*' ... for them that honour me I will honour,
and they that despise me shall be lightly esteemed.'*

~ 1 SAMUEL 2: 30b, KING JAMES VERSION ~

SOME people just seem to be remarkable and the story you're going to hear is about a very remarkable Scotsman. He was remarkable in many ways and many remarkable things were said about him.

Some said, 'he was Scotland's greatest athlete'. Some called him 'the most popular and best loved athlete that Scotland ever produced'. He was called 'the Scottish Superstar of the 1920s' – that lets you know *when* he lived. He was also called 'a traitor to his country'. And, after all that, the famous film 'Chariots of Fire' was made about him.

His name was Eric Henry Liddell. When you hear the story of this man, you will know why he became a legend in his lifetime, and remains a hero and legend now that he is dead. You will understand *why* he was remarkable.

Our Scottish hero was born not in Scotland, but in China, at the beginning of this century. At the time, his father was a Christian missionary there. His mother was a nurse. They were delighted when the healthy little fellow was born.

'We'll call him Henry Eric Liddell,' said his father proudly.

'Henry ... Eric ... Liddell,' repeated his wife slowly. Then she laughed. 'No, I don't think that's a very good name for a Christian missionary's son.'

'Why not?' asked her husband.

'Well, look what the initials spell – H, Henry ... E, Eric ... L for Liddell.'

He laughed too. 'Yes, of course, the children at school would have a bit of fun with that!'

'What about *Eric Henry* Liddell?' she suggested.

And so, Eric Henry Liddell it was.

Little Eric, from the earliest times, loved to run. He loved to take to the hills, bounding up them like a deer, his feet pounding to the rhythm of the words of God in his heart:

They that wait upon the Lord shall renew their strength.
They shall mount up on wings like eagles.

~ ISAIAH 40: 31 ~

At school he proved to be a wonderful sprinter and as the years passed his stride grew stronger and longer and faster and faster. He would throw his head back and his arms would go like pistons, which is why he later became known as 'the Flying Scotsman' – after the fastest steam train of the age. By the time he went to university, his fame had spread.

At Edinburgh University he competed in the 100 yards, the 220 yards and the 440 yards races – what we today call the 100, 200 and 400 metres. He was no longer at school. Now the flower of Scotland's athletes, and competitors from England and abroad, were lined up against him. Undaunted, off he went like a steam train, legs driving, arms pounding. On he thundered to beat the cream of student athletes and become champion in the 100 yards race, and again in the 220 yards. Even in the 440 yards race he came first around the track, head up, his red hair flying in the wind, his eyes on the hills, and God in his lungs.

Eric became Scottish Champion in the 100 and 220 yards races, equalled the Scottish record for the 100 yards, and set a new record time for the 220 yards. He was also capped as a Scottish Rugby inter- nationalist – where Eric 'the Flying Scotsman' played on the left wing. However, it was as an athlete that Eric was known far and wide.

Yet, to Eric, one thing was even more important than his beloved running, more important than anything – his belief in God.

He wanted to tell people about his God, about Jesus. At meetings all over the country, Eric spoke of the love of God. He often talked particularly about Sunday, the Lord's day, saying, 'We should set one day apart for God, Sundays should be special and we should use that day to do good things, to notice the lovely things God has given us, and to rest'. Indeed, Eric Liddell's belief in the importance of Sunday was where the trouble began. You'll hear about this soon.

As time went by, Eric became an even greater sprinter and a match for the crack performers from south of the border.

The year was 1923. The Olympic Games in Paris were a year away. At the Triple 'A' Championships in England, Eric Liddell won the 220 yards sprint and the 100 yards with a new British record that was to stand for 55 years.

And a week later, Eric did something that astonished all the experts in the world of sprinting. He was competing against the best inter- national runners of England and Ireland in the 440 yards sprint. As usual, before the race, he shook hands with all the runners. The com- petitors then got on their marks and, first time, went off with the gun.

They sprinted from the line ... Gillies the English champion and Liddell, stride for stride when ... a gasp from the crowd ... Gillies bumped Liddell and the Scot crashed to the ground. When he raised his head he was well behind the fastest men in Britain. For any normal person that would have been the end of the race. Not for the remarkable Eric Liddell. No, he sprang to his feet and gave chase, legs pounding, arms like pistons ... the Flying Scotsman at full steam. No one believed what they were seeing. It was *impossible* he could catch up. But the glint had come into his eyes ... his head went up as if his heart sang ...

I will lift up mine eyes unto the hills,
from whence cometh my help ....

His feet pounded, his chest pounded.

My help cometh from the Lord
which made heaven and earth.

~ PSALM 121: 1 - 2 ~

His arms drove like pistons; his eyes gazed skywards. He ran like a man inspired. He was gaining ground. The crowd was hushed ... surely this was impossible. And then as the runners burst into the home stretch, they saw Eric draw level with Gillies. They cheered; every voice was with him. He collapsed through the tape, first. Against all odds he had won.

Soon after that Eric received a letter letting him know that he had been selected to run for Britain in the Paris Olympic Games. He was to compete in the 100 metres – a high honour, for the 100 metres was a test of the fastest men in the world and took pride of place in the Games. He was overjoyed. It was a wonderful opportunity. Everyone in Scotland was proud, and full of anticipation. Maybe one of their own Scottish countrymen would be the 'fastest man on earth'!

Then the programme for the Olympic Games was announced. The heats for the 100 metres were on a Sunday and there the real legend of Eric Liddell began.

When Eric read the programme, he simply said, 'I cannot run on a Sunday.' He sent a letter withdrawing from the Games.

People were aghast. 'You are mad to throw up this chance,' they said. 'The chance to be the fastest man on earth, to win a gold medal. To put Scotland on the map.'

'I keep Sunday aside for God,' he said.

'What about your country?' they said. 'You have been selected to represent Britain. You are no better than a traitor to your country.'

'I cannot be a traitor to God,' he said and would not change his mind.

In dismay the Olympic selection committee met. What were they to do? Their finest prospect would not run. At last someone said, 'Let Eric Liddell run the 400 metres. There's no Sunday heats for that race.' And so it was agreed he would compete in the 400 metres, the longest, hardest and most punishing of all the sprints.

It was 1924, a burning hot July day. Paris was crowded with people.

The spectators were awaiting impatiently the final of the 400 metres. Even in the heats the world record had twice been broken and the man who wouldn't run on Sunday had got through to the Olympic finals!

But Eric drew the worst possible position – the dreaded outside lane, where you could not see the other competitors. Inside him were the fastest runners in the world.

Suddenly, through the excited bubbling of the crowd, the sound of the Scottish bagpipes filled the air. The finalists were getting ready, waiting for the starter. Fitch the American world record holder, Butler the British record holder, Imbach the Swiss Champion, Taylor another fast American and, on the outside, Eric Liddell.

The pipes died down. Eric Liddell shook hands with all the competitors. At that moment a man ran up to him and gave him a little note with a message written on it. Eric read the paper and clasped it in his hand. The competitors were called to starter's orders. The whole stadium grew hushed and silent.

The gun cracked! Eric flew from the start ... arms flailing ... legs driving. Half way, he was in the lead. The crowd was frantic. He surely couldn't keep this up. He drove on ... the Englishman was gaining on him ... Fitch, the world record holder, was closing the gap. At fifty metres to go, Eric threw back his head and sped on like a man looking to the hills, inspired by God ... *I will lift up mine eyes unto the hills, from whence cometh my help* ... he drew ahead and, setting a new world record, Eric Liddell broke the tape to the wild cheering of the Olympic crowd.

It was the most popular win of those Olympic Games – probably of any Olympic Games ever.

Eric returned to Scotland to face a hero's welcome in Edinburgh. As his train pulled into the station, he found it crowded with well-wishers. He was jostled and congratulated and cheered, a home-coming to remember for the man who refused to run on Sunday.

When he graduated from university that summer, the principal of the university, who hardly ever cracked a joke, smiled when it came to Eric's turn to graduate. He said, 'Mr Liddell, none can pass you except the examiner.' He was crowned with a laurel crown of victory and carried shoulder high by his fellow students through the town to the kirk of St Giles.

In his honour, the Lord Provost of Edinburgh gave a dinner. Everyone had read or heard of his triumph and everyone was curious to know what was in the note he had been handed before his famous victory. 'Tell us about the note!' they cried.

'Getting that note is one of my finest memories,' he said. 'One of the trainers gave it to me. It came from my favourite book, the Bible. It said, "He that honours me, I shall honour".'

The audience rose to their feet in tribute to this modest man who put his God before fame or popularity, or even his country. Now they understood what had driven this quiet athlete on that hot July day in Paris, what had filled his lungs and given power to his stride. He had been running to honour God.

Now Eric was at the very height of his fame and popularity. The athletics world lay at his feet.

'So Eric, where now? The sky's the limit,' said his friends. 'What will be your next race?'

'China,' said Eric.

'China?' they asked, 'China?!!'

'Yes, China,' said Eric. In his heart he knew that God's next race for him was a different kind. As long and hard and gruelling as the 400 metres and with no cheering crowds this time.

Eric was going to do God's work as a missionary.

So Eric left the fame, the world of athletics and his native Scotland to work with the people of China. As with his running, he gave it everything he had, went full out from the start. And this time the race of his life ran into the full horror of World War II.

Along with thousands of others, separated from his wife and family, Eric was imprisoned by the Japanese. Prison camp needed all his courage, all his stamina and all his faith in God. And that's what he gave it. He worked endlessly and tirelessly, helping other prisoners, organising games for the young folk, comforting the sick and dying. In the end the effort killed this great man.

In 1945, just before the war ended, he collapsed and died. He had done his best for every one. This remarkable man had run to the end of life's race, and when he broke the tape for the last time, I'm sure the angels cheered this winner for God.

24

Old Sarah:
Love Others as Yourself

You shall love your neighbour
as yourself.

~ MATTHEW 22: 39, REVISED STANDARD VERSION ~

NOBODY noticed old Sarah. She seemed to be almost invisible. If there was a dance in the village hall, someone might say later on, 'Was old Sarah at the dance?' and no one could be sure. Perhaps someone might say, 'Oh yes, she was. I remember seeing her picking up empty crisp packets.' Or, 'Oh yes, I saw her helping drunken Johnny into a seat.' But usually people could not remember whether she had been there or not. This was a pity, because she did so many helpful things for other people – like picking up crisp packets and coming to the aid of drunken Johnny.

I suppose one of the strange things about Sarah was her appearance. If you asked one of the locals to describe her, as sure as anything he couldn't. 'Och, she's about middling height, middling build and, well actually ... she's, och ... pretty well invisible.' And that's how she remained until the accident. But you'll hear about that by and by.

There was, at the time of our story, one person who did notice old

Sarah, and that was young Kirsty. Young Kirsty was as noticeable as Sarah was invisible. Everything that Kirsty was, old Sarah was just the opposite.

Kirsty had bright red hair, long and bouncy, a bit like herself. She had bright blue eyes and a skipping way of walking. She was always bursting with stories and laughter, and dressed as brightly as a parrot.

She often visited old Sarah in her cottage. It was almost hidden in a little wood at the edge of the village. Often their conversation went like this:

'Goodness me, girl, goodness me ... what is a pretty young thing like you doing visiting a drab old hen like me?' Sarah would say.

'I like hens,' answered Kirsty. 'They're one of my favourite creatures. They're useful, just like you. And you wouldn't be in the least bit drab if you bothered to look after yourself and wear some bright clothes instead of these old bochles.'

'Och, these suit me fine. No one in their right senses wants to be wasting their time looking at the likes of me.'

'Well, I'm in my right senses,' is all that Kirsty would say. But to be honest she was quite angry because Kirsty knew a lot about Sarah that no one else knew. She knew, for instance, that Sarah weeded old Hector's vegetable patch after he was in bed and the whole village fast asleep. And Kirsty also knew that when Sarah was a little girl of ten, her mother died and Sarah looked after her little brother and her two little sisters and their father.

Kirsty also knew that both of Sarah's sisters had married and her brother went to sea and was never heard of again. Her father became old, bad-tempered and full of demands like, 'Hurry up with that tea, Sarah. Are you growing it or what?' And complaints like, 'This tea's as cold as death. Are you trying to kill me or what?' And, 'This scrambled egg's made of leather. Do you want to make me sick or what?' And so, of course, it was Sarah who had to look after the old man as he grew more unpleasant and more insulting as the years passed. He even died complaining that he didn't expect the tea in heaven would be much better.

'I would have put salt in his tea and given him burnt toast and cold custard and soggy cabbage,' Kirsty used to think when she heard about the dreadful old man.

So she wanted her friend to enjoy life now that she was old. No wonder Kirsty got angry when Sarah said it was a waste of time to visit the likes of her.

It was last winter when Kirsty first began to notice that Sarah was acting strangely. She seemed to be very slow in everything she did. She also seemed thinner and paler and, if it were possible, even *more* invisible. 'Are you eating enough? You look as thin as a needle,' Kirsty would say.

'Don't you be bothering about me,' Sarah muttered.

'You should look after yourself.'

'Och, I'm fine.'

'You're pale.'

'I'm alright.'

'You're thin. I've brought you some biscuits.'

'That's kind, I'll keep them till later.'

When Kirsty visited old Sarah, the thing she loved most was when the old lady taught her to play the harp. Sarah played beautifully. Her favourite tune was one of the first that she had learned as a little girl. It was called 'The Spinning Wheel'. Sometimes Sarah used to sing it in her old thin voice.

On the night before the accident, Sarah was playing this tune. A little fire was glowing in the grate and it was really cosy. Sarah looked very frail sitting there, with her thin hands like graceful birds making lovely sad music on the harp. But Kirsty saw a tear running down Sarah's face when she sang the words, 'Sounds the sweet voice of a young maiden singing'.

She stopped playing suddenly, and said, 'Kirsty, if anything happens to me, I would like you to have this harp. Now run along – it's dark and cold and time you were home'.

Kirsty, for once, didn't know what to say, so home she went. But she couldn't get out of her mind the picture of Sarah's pale tired face and the tears in the old woman's eyes. Always, too, she seemed to hear the old woman's voice singing the last slow chorus of the song:

Slower and slower and slower the wheel swings;
Lower and lower and lower the reel rings,
Ere the wheel and the reel stop their ringing and moving
Through the grove the young lovers by moonlight are roving.

123

That night was wet and windy. Kirsty couldn't sleep at first, but when she did eventually, she dreamt she was in a dark wood, listening to a strange wailing scream like an animal in pain. And then she saw it *was* an animal caught in a trap. Going closer she saw that it was old Sarah's beautiful harp, held in the steel teeth of a trap. The harp was screaming. Kirsty awoke and the night seemed to last forever.

Morning finally came. Kirsty did not wait for breakfast, but ran all the way to the cottage. As she approached, she found a trail of blood – she followed it fearfully.

The door of Sarah's cottage was ajar. Kirsty pushed it open and found her friend lying on the floor. At least Sarah was still breathing. Kirsty threw a blanket over her and ran like the wind to the doctor's house.

For three days old Sarah lay between life and death, saying nothing. Then, on the evening of the third day, she croaked out, 'Old Hector … must help old Hector …. ' Then she fell asleep again.

That was how the whole story came to light and how old Hector's life was saved as well. This is how it happened. All that winter Sarah had been visiting the old man. He was housebound and Sarah had been feeding him from the few stores she had herself, while she grew weaker and weaker, until that very night when Kirsty last saw her.

It was, you'll remember, a cold windy night. Sarah had left her cottage to make her way through the dark to Hector's house. But she never actually got there. For she had just crossed the bridge over the river when a gust of wind carried her frail body right into the path of a passing truck. Sarah was so light that the driver didn't even feel the impact. Luckily, it was just a glancing blow, but it left her unconscious and bleeding. She crawled home when she came to and that is where Kirsty found her 'in the nick of time', as the doctor said. And old Hector, too, was at death's door when they found him. So that, in a way, is how Kirsty came to save two lives at once.

Now we are near the end of our story, but not quite – for Kirsty also performed a miracle! None of the village people would have believed it was possible. For Kirsty also made old Sarah *visible* – not only visible, but as colourful as a peacock.

You see, Sarah became well again and returned to her old self. And one day, soon after, Kirsty was visiting her at the cottage. It was then that Kirsty first noticed the words written above the old woman's mantlepiece: *Love your neighbour as yourself.*

'What are you staring at, girl?' asked old Sarah.

'The words above your mantlepiece,' said Kirsty, 'It says, *Love your neighbour as yourself.*'

'That's right,' said old Sarah. 'Good advice from the Good Book.'

'But *you* don't follow it!' burst out Kirsty.

'Well girl, I try ... nobody's perfect,' said the old lady quietly.

'No you don't ... you love your neighbour, yes. But look at *you*. You don't love *you*. You don't look after *you*. You nearly got yourself killed looking after old Hector. But who would've looked after him if you had died? And I ... I don't want you dead! You're as thin as a scarecrow, and just look at you – grey and black clothes – you don't need to dress dowdy just cos you're old. That's no excuse! You're just about invisible, and ... well, I'm *not* sorry for saying all this ... !'

Kirsty, red in the face and amazed at herself, ran out of the cottage and all the way home, thinking, 'Oh dear, that's done it ... now I've lost Sarah as my friend.'

But next afternoon, as soon as school was finished, Kirsty couldn't help it – she just had to hurry round to see her old friend. 'But I'm not going to say I'm sorry,' she said to herself.

When she got there, Sarah called out, 'Well, well, child ... come in.'

Kirsty walked in and was astonished. On the table was a beautiful cake and a lovely white linen tablecloth and places set for two people. But, most astonishing of all, was the appearance of old Sarah. She was brightly, almost dazzlingly, dressed in orange and yellow and blue!

'Is this bright enough for you?' she asked. 'It's my birthday, so I decided to treat myself to a birthday party and a few new clothes. I was expecting you. Sit down and we'll begin.'

From that day on, Sarah was no longer invisible.

If you are ever passing through a certain Scottish village and see a cheerful old woman dressed as brightly as a rainbow, you might be looking at Sarah ....

25

God be with You

*'To have good fruit you must have a healthy tree;
if you have a poor tree, you will have bad fruit.
A tree is known by the kind of fruit it bears.'*

~ MATTHEW 12: 33, GOOD NEWS BIBLE ~

OUR story begins during a leafy summer not very long ago. School was over for the day in the little Scottish village of Kilbracken. The three pals walked down the village street. For once they were all quiet – they were all thinking and they were all hiding tears. Who would have believed that, today of all days, they would have lumps in their throats, far less tears in their eyes.

'Especially me,' thought Alan. He kept his curly, dark head down as he looked at his misty feet, hoping that Caroline and Wendy wouldn't notice. But Caroline and Wendy were busy with their own thoughts.

This was the day that they had all looked forward to. They had talked about it for weeks. The last day of term, their very last day at Primary School, the end of Primary 7 – freedom!

'And here I am,' thought Caroline, 'bubbling like a kid in Primary 1 on the very first day of school!'

'Let's go and climb our tree,' suggested Wendy. Without a word the others followed her along the path by the river to their special meeting-place.

They were all good climbers and scrambled up into their own favourite perch on a branch of their favourite tree. From there they looked down into the pool where Caroline and Alan had done a life-saving job on Wendy's kitten when it fell in. In fact, that was how they all came to be friends in the first place. But that is another story. For now, they all looked down into the pool and thought about the future. And they were thinking about the future not just because it was the last day of term, but because of the words that were still ringing like fading bells in their ears.

At the end of the service that morning, the headmistress had dismissed every class in the school except Primary 7. They were left, one little class standing in the big hall.

The Headmistress, Mrs Campbell, said, 'I have a surprise for you all. Follow me.' And she led the class out of the school, down the street and into the only hotel in the village. She led them upstairs and stood before a door. 'Now, in you go.' she said.

There in front of them was a table, with names written on cards in front of each place – the names of every single child in the class. The names were neatly written by hand and they at once recognised the handwriting. They had all copied that writing when they were in Primary 1. It was the careful handwriting of Mrs Campbell.

'Eat as much as you like,' she told them.

It was indeed a feast, a *wonderful* feast.

But it was not the food that brought tears to the eyes of Alan, Caroline and Wendy. No, it was Mrs Campbell's story. She could always tell a good story.

After they had eaten as much as they possibly could – and in some cases a little more – Mrs Campbell had said to them, 'Primary 7, I want to give you all something to take away with you. I am going to give you one last story from me. A story is better than any toy because you can keep it forever. It will never break or wear out and you can give it away and still keep it. Indeed, the more often you give it away, the better it gets. This story is especially for you.

'Perhaps you won't know this, but today is a special occasion for me as well as you. You are my very last Primary 7. Like you, I am leaving, so today is goodbye. That is why we are having this feast together.

'Well, I lay in bed last night and wondered what I could say to you. While I was thinking, I fell asleep ... and when I was sleeping, I had a dream. I am going to tell you about my dream.

'In my dream I became as light as air. I was a space traveller. My mission was to visit many planets and find out what their customs were. Of all the planets I observed, one memory is more vivid than all the rest – it is of my brief visit to the little planet of Womantu.

'I landed at the space platform and asked directions from one of the local people. There was something very beautiful and strangely familiar about his face, but at the time I couldn't make out what it was. Then I made my way on foot to the centre of the town. It seemed like the whole town was gathered together for some kind of ceremony. All the townspeople were clad in long cloaks of undyed hand-woven cloth. The cloaks were very plain, plain grey, and all similar in design and colour. I asked a friendly young man beside me, whose face was also strangely familiar, the reason for the gathering.

'He told me: "It is called the Transformation of the Cloak, a ceremony of Goodbye." Then I saw that it was a kind of funeral, because there, laid out upon an altar of stone, was the body of a very old man. He too wore a plain cloak. Beneath it I realised that his clothes were shabby and threadbare. Clearly this man had been very poor. The lad told me that the old man had been a carpenter.

'I then asked the lad about the cloaks. He said that every inhabitant of that place was given a cloak the moment they were born. The cloaks grew as they grew. The cloaks were always clean and had a beautiful light scent like wild summer flowers.

'As I was talking to this young man, I became aware of a growing murmuring amongst the crowd ... an *excited* murmuring. I turned in the direction of the old man on the altar. And, Primary 7, an amazing sight met my eyes. For as if sewn by invisible hands, beautiful embroidery began to appear and shimmer on the cloak of the old man. Everyone watched in silence as marvellous patterns and designs began to appear in colours of red and blue and gold, beautiful colours and patterns, until it seemed that the face of the old man shone, even in death.

'Well, every square of the cloak shimmered like silk and bore this marvellous embroidery. I was completely astonished, Primary 7, and, as you can imagine, quite curious – so I asked the lad beside me if this always happened. The youth laughed.

'"Oh no, no," he said. "Sometimes the cloak falls into tatters; sometimes little patches of embroidery appear; and sometimes it's just an awful mess. This is a very ancient ceremony," he added. "The wise folk say that the colours and embroidery tell the story of the dead person's life. Look there ..., " he pointed at the cloak of the dead man, "Red and Blue and Gold. They say *Red* is for courage and *Blue* for honesty and *Gold* for love. You see, this old man has lived a very good life .... "

'Just then we were interrupted by a great clapping and chanting. The people were applauding the old man's cloak as if it were the end of a great theatre performance. Some were even cheering, and chanting "God be with you! God be with you! Goodbye! Goodbye!"

'But then it became "Goodbye and Hello! Goodbye and Hello!"

'I asked the lad why. He looked at me as though I were simpleminded and said, "Don't you know that every Goodbye is also a Hello?"

'Suddenly I saw the sun going down over a distant hill, and when I looked round again the young man was gone – and the crowd and everything. My dream was gone too. The last thing I heard was the sun whispering "Hello". I awoke and there was the sun like a red glow, shining out of a blue sky, turning the walls of my room gold.

'And so, Primary 7, I knew that this story was for you – it is my Goodbye to you. I have seen you all from the time you arrived in Primary 1, with your shining faces, clean and new. Seven years ago it was, Primary 7, more than *half* your lives ago! And now you have most of your lives ahead of you ... as I have most of my life behind me.

'Well, to finish with, there is one thing I didn't tell you about my dream, Primary 7. The reason I found the faces of the townspeople of Womantu familiar was because the faces were *your* faces, Primary 7, *your* faces. You are all stories waiting to be told .... '

Mrs Campbell got up out of her chair at that point and walked over to the door, whispering, 'Remember, Primary 7 – *Red* and *Blue* and best of all *Gold*. Goodbye my children, goodbye Primary 7, God be with you ... God be with you all!'

And with that, like a dream, she was gone. Primary 7 were left in the room, all alone and feeling somehow sad. But it was as if Mrs

Campbell had some magical touch, because as they sat there the sun suddenly burst into the room. That is when Wendy and Caroline and Alan left and walked silently down the village street, along the path and up into their tree above the pool.

In the pool the sun was shining, burning like gold.

'Where do you think Mrs Campbell went?' asked Wendy.

'I expect she went to say hello to someone,' said Alan.

'What do you think she meant by the Red and Blue and Gold?' Wendy persisted.

From the topmost branch of the tree, Caroline's voice drifted down. 'I think Mrs Campbell's very crafty, very clever – because when we go to the Senior School, that's when these colours appear .... '

'How do you mean?' quibbled Alan.

'Well, the school uniform is grey and the tie of Kinglamnock High School is .... '

'*Red, Blue* and *Gold,*' chorused the other two.

'It's a bit frightening, the big school,' said Wendy.

'Well, Red is for courage,' said Alan.

'Blue's for honesty and Gold's for love,' added Wendy.

'Well, maybe it won't be so bad, after all. There's a swimming pool there ... yes and all kinds of new people to say hello to ... I think it could be great. I wonder if we'll learn embroidery .... '